The
Witch's
Way Home

The
Witch's
Way Home

*Magic, Spells and Rituals to Lead
You Back to Your Most Powerful Self*

EMMA GRIFFIN

HAY HOUSE

Carlsbad, California • New York City
London • Sydney • New Delhi

Published in the United Kingdom by:
Hay House UK Ltd, The Sixth Floor, Watson House,
54 Baker Street, London W1U 7BU
Tel: +44 (0)20 3927 7290; www.hayhouse.co.uk

Published in the United States of America by:
Hay House LLC, PO Box 5100, Carlsbad, CA 92018-5100
Tel: (1) 760 431 7695 or (800) 654 5126; www.hayhouse.com

Published in Australia by:
Hay House Australia Publishing Pty Ltd, 18/36 Ralph St, Alexandria NSW 2015
Tel: (61) 2 9669 4299; www.hayhouse.com.au

Published in India by:
Hay House Publishers (India) Pvt Ltd, Muskaan Complex,
Plot No.3, B-2, Vasant Kunj, New Delhi 110 070
Tel: (91) 11 4176 1620; www.hayhouse.co.in

A catalogue record for this book is available from the British Library.

Tradepaper ISBN: 978-1-4019-7625-5
E-book ISBN: 978-1-83782-125-9
Audiobook ISBN: 978-1-83782-124-2

Interior images: Shutterstock

Interior image designer, p1, 57, 115, 169, 219: Kam Bains

10 9 8 7 6 5 4 3 2 1

Printed in the United States of America

This product uses responsibly sourced papers and/or recycled materials. For more information, see www.hayhouse.com.

In a world that often dismisses the mystical and the unexplained, finding solace in one's own identity as a witch can be a daunting journey. Throughout history, witches have been misunderstood and persecuted, their power feared by those who fail to comprehend its true nature. It is for this reason that I dedicate this book to all those who have felt lost, yearning to return home to themselves as the witches they have always been.

Within these pages lies ancient wisdom and modern insights, carefully curated to serve as a guiding light for those of you seeking your path. It is my hope that this book will empower you to embrace your inner magic, reminding you of the strength and beauty that lies within.

May it be a beacon of hope for those of you who feel isolated or marginalized in your beliefs; may it provide comfort during moments of doubt or uncertainty; and, most importantly, may it inspire you to reclaim your power and find solace in your unique connection with the universe.

For all of you brave souls ready to embark on this transformative journey, I offer my deepest gratitude and support. Together, let us celebrate our shared heritage as witches and embrace the enchantment that resides within us all.

Contents

List of Spells, Rituals and Exercises

Introduction

The reason I have written this book is because this is the guide I wish I had had when I started my path in witchcraft, over 20 years ago.

The Witch's Way Home will serve as a compass, leading you back to your authentic essence. It will unveil the hidden realms within and around you, reminding you that there is more to life than meets the eye. This is not just another self-help book; it is an invitation to rediscover yourself and live authentically as a witch. Through its roadmap for personal growth, spiritual awakening and living a magical life, this book aims to guide you back home – back to the path of your true self, to the witch you came here to be.

As a witch, it is crucial to understand the interconnectedness of all things, and the profound impact it can have on your life. The natural world, for instance, holds immense power and wisdom that can be tapped into for guidance and manifestation. By immersing yourself in the beauty of forests, mountains, or even your own garden or local park, you can attune yourself to the rhythms of nature and align your intentions with its flow. Throughout this book, I will share with you ancient wisdom passed down from generations of witches and guide you on a journey to harness the energy of the universe, tapping into dimensions that are often unseen but ever-present. By delving into these dimensions, you will discover hidden truths about yourself and your place in the world. You will learn how to receive signs and guidance, and how to align your intentions with the natural flow of energy in the world around, and within you. By learning how to work with nature and different energies and vibrations, you can create a harmonious balance within yourself and attract abundance into your life. This process involves honing your intuition, practising visualization techniques, and utilizing various rituals that resonate with your intentions, all of which we'll cover in these pages.

Embarking on the journey of witchcraft also offers a profound opportunity for self-discovery and empowerment. This journey not only offers practical rituals and ceremonies, such as moon ceremonies and empowerment spells, but it also provides a path to understanding your innate abilities and potential. By honing these skills and embracing your unique gifts, you can navigate life's challenges with clarity and purpose. In essence, practising witchcraft offers a chance to find your way home – a path back to yourself and a deeper connection with the world around you.

Having a journal and pen nearby is essential for this journey, as it allows you to record your experiences, insights and manifestations along the way. Through reflection and introspection, you can track your progress, deepen your understanding and continue to grow on your path as a witch.

Throughout this book, I will also share personal anecdotes, life lessons and insights that have shaped my own journey of witchcraft. I believe that, by sharing these experiences, we can learn from each other's journeys and grow together as a community.

My Personal Journey

My journey to becoming a witch has always been within me, deep in my soul. Having a past life as a witch and growing up in a magical household, you could compare my family and our lifestyle to characters from a *Harry Potter* book. When I was a young child, my mother would make me spell jars, create stories about witches and teach me the power of nature, the magic of plants and the changes in the seasons. We would sit in the garden watching the moon and she would explain to me how the moon influences us. My mother was a witch, so this is really where my journey began.

My father was more spiritual than magical. He worked in the fashion industry for most of his career and his roles involved travel, which gave him the opportunity to visit many countries all over the world. This led to a fascination with different cultures, particularly those with strong spiritual beliefs, and, in turn, through meeting people with varying beliefs, he found a love for meditation. He expanded my awareness to the universe and meditation.

From the age of four, I saw and talked to spirits and beings who are non-human. Although I had no idea that these people were not physical, I would always tell my parents and they never discouraged me, which I think has helped me keep this strong connection to the spirit world as an adult.

During my mid-teens, I grew less interested in the magical way of life and followed the 'normal' world of education and fitting in. Despite this, I've always been able to see auras and loved watching the colours change around people. Again, I had no idea that this was not something everyone could see, and when I mentioned what I could do to my friends, they mocked it and made fun of me, which of course made me draw inwards.

Often as a family we would have a séance after our Sunday roast. We would all sit around the table with a large white candle in the centre. All the lights would be turned off and my mother would hold space and guide us all. Sometimes the table would move or lift at the corners. I never thought this wasn't 'normal' and assumed that all families did the same on a Sunday. My mother would also make Ouija boards that she would only do with my father and her friends. She was a gifted tarot reader, too; I watched her with fascination as she would give family members readings at the start of the new year.

I didn't personally find witchcraft until I visited a large UK spiritual fair and had a tarot reading. During this reading, I was told that I was never going to be able to have children. Looking back, I feel very strongly that this isn't something a practitioner should relay to the sitter. At the time, I was incredibly upset – I knew that I was going to marry my boyfriend Steve, and I so desperately wanted to be a mother.

After the fair I was worried about what I had been told and decided to borrow all my mother's witchcraft books and work on some spells to fall pregnant. It was a little overwhelming at first as there was so much variation in practices. My hope was to find one book that could show me exactly how it should be done. Once I had decided on which path appealed to me, it was time to begin researching. My mother always told me, 'A witch never stops learning; there are always new things to study and new pathways of interest.'

Most of her books were based on Wiccan beliefs (a modern pagan religious movement centred around nature worship and practising rituals to connect with spiritual energies), so I started by following that path and practised every day. I made two altars: one in the heart of our home and one in our bedroom, focusing on healing from the message the tarot reader had told me, performing empowerment and fertility magic the whole time. Steve would often come home to me brewing interesting-smelling potions on our stove. I would make bath rituals for us both and ask him to carry around charms that I had enchanted. I also started to honour the moon phases. I fell pregnant nine months later and gave birth to my daughter and, three years later, my son.

This was the first moment in my life when witchcraft returned me home to my true self. I had gathered everything I had learned from this journey, using all my life experiences mixed in with my mother's guidance that had been passed down through generations, and whatever else resonated with me.

As I write this book, I am now in my late forties. Looking back at my journey, I have encountered numerous challenges that have shaped me into the person I am today – from battling cancer to facing near-death experiences and enduring the loss of both my parents, life has tested me in unimaginable ways. However, it is during these darker times that I discovered my true calling as a witch. I uncovered the dimensions that were within me and around me that I could tap into for support, healing and wisdom.

Embracing the path of witchcraft has not only helped me find solace and strength within myself, but has also been instrumental in saving my life. The practice of witchcraft has provided me with a sense of empowerment and connection to the natural world around me. It is this that compelled me to write this book – to teach you all that I have learned, with everything taking you back home to the witch within.

Through psychological transformation, spiritual awakening and reclaiming my personal power, I have found solace and empowerment within the realm of witchcraft. Through rituals, spells and divination practices, I have gained a renewed sense of self-worth and purpose. The act of casting spells has allowed me to manifest positive change in my life while providing an outlet for emotional release. I have come to realize that being a witch is not about conforming to societal norms or seeking validation from others. Instead, it is about embracing our true selves and connecting with the ancient wisdom that resides within us.

My journey on this path came with a lot of research and learning and, of course, being guided by my mother. However, I also had a lot of years of healing – healing myself and doing the work to get to know who I was, what I loved and what I valued, and to find my authentic self. I feel it is important to really understand yourself before becoming a witch, and I will guide you through this as we journey through the book together.

I also began to recognize the interconnectedness between all living beings, and have always strived to live in harmony with nature. I learned how to look inwards for guidance and how to rely on the natural world for support. In doing so, I found I could unlock my full potential and create magic in my life. By drawing upon this energy, I am able to maintain a balance between giving and receiving – giving back to the universe in order to receive its energy. This can be done through acts of kindness, gratitude or simply taking care of oneself.

As a witch, I have come to understand that empowerment is not just about external strength or success, but rather an inner journey of self-discovery and connection. Throughout history, women have been marginalized and silenced, their voices suppressed and their power diminished. My mission is to change this narrative, empowering women to embrace their unique gifts, stand in their truth and be an advocate for themselves and others.

Remember to shine your light – the world needs it now more than ever.

In a world filled with distractions and noise, finding one's true self can be an arduous journey. However, the path of the witch offers solace and guidance, leading us back to our authentic essence. *The Witch's Way Home* serves as a compass. Through its teachings, you will learn to harness the energy that resides within, unlocking your untapped potential. With each step taken on this mystical journey, you inch closer to rediscovering your true self. Embracing the wisdom of *The Witch's Way Home* will illuminate your path and ultimately lead you back home – to the witch you are.

PART I

Starting Your Path

This is where your journey begins – where you will learn about the word 'witch' and all that it entails. When you first step onto this path, it can feel scary. You might fear what others will think of you or worry that you may do something wrong. However, this journey is yours alone to undertake. Do not let the opinions or judgements of others dictate how you explore your spirituality. Instead, focus on finding what resonates with you personally – what brings you joy, peace and fulfilment.

This first part of the book unravels the enigmatic world of witches. Delving deep into their essence, you will uncover the true meaning of what it means to be a witch and any fears that may be holding you back. As you embark on this exploration, you will be comforted by the realization that you are not alone in your path; most of us carry a hidden trauma known as the 'witch wound', which we will unveil and come to understand.

But fear not, for within these pages lies a comprehensive how-to guide that will empower you to embrace your inner witch. From casting a circle and grounding your energy to exploring all the tools of a witch, my guidance will illuminate your way towards harnessing your full potential as a witch.

CHAPTER 1

Embracing Your Inner Witch

While, in recent years, the word 'witch' has caused quite a stir on social media and has become a huge trend globally, witches have been a source of fascination and fear throughout history. Witches are also very misunderstood. When people ask me what I do, I answer that I am a professional witch and, with that, they usually laugh, as though I am joking. A common response I get is, 'Well, you don't look like a witch', but what does a witch look like? People's reactions often come from a deep-seated fear or uneasiness of witches, shaped by how they are depicted in the movies and in fairy tales. In this chapter, I want to share with you what it means to be a witch and why it isn't anything like those stereotypes. We'll also explore what might be holding you back from embracing the witch within.

What Is a Witch?

In reality, there is no one answer to this question. The concept of a witch varies greatly depending on cultural and historical context, and what brings us to witchcraft will vary from person to person. Some people may have a deep calling; some may have been inspired by witches or something they've seen on social media or in a movie. Some people are born into mystical families, while others have natural abilities. Some join covens to work with other witches, and some prefer to work by themselves. Some witches may only practise for a few months and then never again, but have still called themselves a witch. I personally believe that anyone can be a witch and the path is personal to the individual.

Witchcraft is the practice of using personal energy and intention to bring about desired changes in the world. There are hundreds of different kinds of witches (*the most common of which we'll explore in Chapter 15*), and witchcraft traditions can vary wildly from place to person. Contrary to what the movies show and what is in a lot of books, a witch is not a green-faced, hunched-back woman with a huge nose and warts, who wears a black pointy hat, dresses only in black, rides her broomstick at night cursing others and poisons princesses with her black magic.

On the contrary, witches align themselves with the natural elements, such as earth, air, fire and water, and can channel their energy to achieve desired outcomes; whether that is healing ailments or manifesting abundance in their lives, witches rely on magic to bring about positive change. I perceive magic as a means of self-discovery and personal growth. Through practising witchcraft and engaging in magical rituals, I delve deep into my subconscious mind and explore hidden aspects of myself. This introspection allows me to gain insight into my strengths and weaknesses while fostering self-awareness.

Whenever anyone asks me what I think a witch is, I always reply with the same answer: for me, a witch is a wise woman (or man) who is unapologetically rooted in their power, living their life completely on their own terms. A witch lives and works in harmony with nature, in touch with plants and animals, connected to their inner magic, and knows how to work with their power to bring about change in the world.

When you feel a calling to return home to yourself as a witch, it could 'trigger' you and bring up fears within you. I want to spend some time now exploring why this is the case.

The Witch Wound

Within my practice as a witch, I work mainly with women from all around the world. I guide them to live their most magical life and step into their authentic self. However, 95 per cent of my clients struggle collectively with one thing – and that is the fear of judgement from others. For many, this is not the fear of judgement from their loved ones, but from other women. I have also had this deep fear and I am sure many of you are holding this fear within yourself too. I believe that this fear comes from the witch wound, but also from the world around us.

The witch wound is a collective trauma that manifests today as a fear of being seen, speaking up and stepping into your own magic, and of being judged by others. The fear, grief and shame of our ancestors have all been passed down through the years.

This fear of being judged comes from the 'Burning Times', the great witch hunt that lasted from the 15th to the 18th century. During this time, thousands of people were accused of witchcraft and were killed as the Church saw witchcraft as a threat to its power and authority. Women who were believed to practise magic, or who practised alternative forms of spirituality or healing, were often accused of being in league with the devil.

Many of these women who were accused of witchcraft were actually healers or midwives who provided essential care for their communities. Thousands of innocent women and men were executed in the most inhuman and brutal of ways: burning, beheading, drowning and hanging.

The accusations often stemmed from rumours or personal grudges, and confessions were frequently obtained through torture. The Burning Times didn't just affect witches; it affected everyone within the community – men, women and children. Eventually, women learned that it was safer to stay quiet than to speak up or stand out with their own uniqueness. They were forced to betray each other and 'out' other women in their community. These women were sisters and friends, but they feared the torture and persecution, so betrayed each other to protect themselves. This fear is still deep within women today.

Those who stood by and watched the witches burn – whether they supported what was happening or not – had a mark left on their consciousness. This mark has gone through the generations of our ancestors and imprinted itself onto our DNA.

How the Witch Wound Manifests in the World Today

This witch wound has forced our feminine gifts to be kept locked away, to be belittled, through fear, guilt and shame. Society has programmed us to disconnect from our own selves, from nature and from each other.

Although women are no longer burned at the stake as witches, the witch wound has left a lasting impact on society, as it has expanded the belief that women are inherently evil and untrustworthy. Women who are outspoken or assertive or who exhibit traits such as independence, intelligence and confidence, are often labelled as 'witches' and are subjected to harassment or discrimination. Women who practise alternative forms of spirituality or healing are often dismissed as 'new age' or 'woo-woo'.

Today, the witch wound can be seen in various forms. I have witnessed many women who are living in fear of being different, showing their uniqueness and stopping themselves from going towards their true desires. This wound manifests for women by playing small, fearing being seen and judged, and worrying about receiving nasty remarks from other women. The witch wound doesn't just affect our relationship with ourselves and our magic, it affects our relationship with all the women around us – withholding negative feelings, competing, comparing and feeling threatened or envious.

Furthermore, social media has amplified this mentality by allowing people to spread false information and rumours about others. This can lead to cyberbullying and harassment, causing emotional harm to those targeted.

This is sad because so many women are not moving in alignment with their true selves. Instead, they believe their fears and stay grounded in their past. So many women feel incapable of success – the world seems daunting, so many prefer to remain playing small.

Over the page are just a few of the symptoms of the trauma many of us still carry in the form of the witch wound:

● You feel the need to keep your social circles small.

● You mistrust other women.

● You are always looking to please others.

● You struggle with feeling at home within.

● You have irrational fears of drowning, hanging and fire.

● You repeat patterns of victimhood, such as betrayal and trauma.

● You hide your spiritual beliefs and magical practices from others.

● You are afraid to speak your mind and express your emotions.

● You feel constantly judged for being different.

● You experience feelings of doubt, guilt and shame about your intuitive abilities.

● You are secretive about using your healing abilities and owning your magic.

● You hold a mistrust of authority figures.

● You are constantly worried about being hurt by others.

● You are self-sabotaging your own joy so as not to upset others.

Do you recognize any of these traits in yourself?

Societal pressure, media influence, cultural norms, fear of judgement and gender stereotypes all contribute to the difficulty for women to step into their authentic selves. These negative portrayals have extended harmful stereotypes about witches that still exist today. We continue to see the demonization of women who are seen as 'other' or different, and many people still associate witchcraft with Satanism or black magic. But living authentically means being true to yourself, embracing your values and not conforming to societal pressures or expectations. It means prioritizing personal wellbeing over external perceptions. Take a moment to ask yourself now, 'Am I living my authentic life?'

Embrace the unknown, for it is through facing our fears that we find true courage.

How the Witch Wound Affected Me

For me, the witch wound first appeared in my life by keeping the word witch a secret. I felt I had to separate my 'witch' lifestyle and my career (I had started my own business as an editorial photographer, working in mainly fashion photography and content creation for global brands). My mother always told me to keep it private and not to be seen because of the fallout I would receive from others. My father didn't like witchcraft – he felt it was evil and not to be messed with – so this also made me remain small as I was afraid of being judged, rejected or mocked by the people around me.

As a child at school, I was always told I was odd, silly or crazy by the other kids, and how strange my mother was. This fear caused me to dim my own light, to silence my truth and hide my passions to keep my magical lifestyle as a witch private. It also caused me to doubt my own inner wisdom.

I separated the 'photographer' and the 'witch'. On photoshoots I would often give models crystals or I would relay guidance I was hearing and feeling, but I never told them I was channeling; instead they thought I was wise!

I have come so far in my journey to heal my own personal traumas and the witch wound, but I still struggle with being seen and still hold the fear of judgement from other women. It was only when my parents passed that I 'came out', so to speak, to the world. I felt powerful. I felt strong, but I also felt that I had helped my ancestors by claiming that word and that wound. By standing in my power and 'coming out' as a witch, I was then authentically seen. This changed me in so many ways because what I feared would happen didn't; I didn't get mocked – instead, I have gained more clarity about my purpose and how best to use my gifts to help others in the world. I have also come to truly accept and love all the parts of myself that I used to find it difficult to face.

It's time to move away from negative stereotypes and embrace the diversity within alternative forms of spirituality. By doing so, we can begin to heal the witch wound and create a more inclusive society where everyone is free to practise their beliefs without fear of discrimination or persecution.

How to Fight Against the Witch Wound

I feel that the first step in healing the witch wound is to acknowledge its existence. For too long, our culture has downplayed the significance of this historical trauma. We have been taught that witches were evil, dangerous creatures who deserved punishment for their crimes. This narrative has been perpetuated through literature, movies and other forms of media that depict witches as villains or objects of fear.

One way to promote healing is to speak out against injustice and support each other in order to create a more equitable world. Our nature, our uniqueness, our wisdom and our essence are not a threat or something that needs to be judged or questioned. Speak your truth, from a place of love, and stand up for others. It is time for us to honour our ancestors who suffered at the hands of patriarchal systems that sought to suppress feminine power! Call it out when you see someone judged harshly, segregated or oppressed.

We must also teach our children about gender equality and respect for all individuals, regardless of their gender identity. We must strive to understand each other's differences and celebrate them rather than fear them. By doing so, we can lead more fulfilling lives and inspire others to do the same.

Society must also play its part by challenging traditional gender norms and creating an environment that encourages women's empowerment and self-expression. We need to understand that traditional witchcraft practices – such as working with nature and its cycles, celebrating seasonal festivals and conducting rituals to honour the Earth and its elements – are not evil, but instead are a way for individuals to connect with their spirituality and the natural world around them. Only then can we create a society that is truly accepting of all individuals.

In my mind, social media could be a wonderful source of information because people can learn in so many more ways than ever before. They can be inspired, meet like-minded witches and learn together. I wish I'd had this body of information at 22 when I started on this path. Social media should be used as a force for good – there is such potential for an online worldwide community of witches, bringing together women from all over the world who are being called to this sacred part of themselves that has been repressed and punished for centuries.

By acknowledging the witch wound and working towards healing it, women can reclaim their power and embrace their true selves. By doing so, we can create a better future for ourselves and generations to come.

How to Begin to Embrace the Witch Within

When we heal our witch wound, we become confident in who we are and are no longer so vulnerable to the thoughts and opinions of others. It is not just about standing in our power or being seen or heard, though. It is about honouring our ancestors – the women who died for their magic, their wisdom and their power.

In recent years, many women have reclaimed the word witch as a symbol of power and independence. To claim it into your life means to embrace your inner strength and connect with the natural world around you.

One way to do this is by exploring the history and mythology surrounding witches. Learning about the powerful women who were persecuted for their beliefs can help you feel connected to a long line of strong, independent women who refused to be silenced. As a witch you are deeply connected to your lineage. By exploring family histories and traditions, while seeking guidance from those who came before you in the spirit world, you can access invaluable insights that inform your spiritual practices. This exploration enables you to forge a profound connection with your roots while honouring the wisdom passed down through the generations.

Another way to claim the word witch is by practising rituals that honour nature and celebrate your own power. This could include lighting candles, meditating or creating altars that reflect your personal beliefs and values (we'll explore how to do this in the chapters that follow). Ultimately, claiming the word witch for your life means embracing your unique identity and using it to make positive changes in the world around you. By connecting with nature and honouring your inner strength, you can become a force for good in a world that so desperately needs it.

I feel that one of the strongest ways to start to heal your witch wound is to learn practices that bring you back to your mind, body and soul – practices that regulate your nervous system. All the feelings of being different and unsafe live in your body within your emotions. Once you can heal these emotions, you will start to find safety within yourself. The ritual below will help you to do just that.

HEALING THE WITCH WOUND RITUAL

Here is your first ritual that will help you take your first step on the path to beginning to heal your witch wound. Remember, this is an ongoing journey.

The perfect time for this ritual is: full moon.

TOOLS

We will explore the tools of the witch in Chapter 3. For now, for this ritual you will need the following items:

- ❯ matches
- ❯ a candle: this can be a simple tea light, dinner or pillar candle
- ❯ a journal so you can make notes
- ❯ incense to cleanse
- ❯ a pen and a piece of A4 paper
- ❯ a fireproof container

INSTRUCTIONS

1. On a full moon, take some time to sit on the ground outside, under the moon or next to a window.

2. Light the candle.

3. Now, in your journal, reflect on what the witch wound means to you. Ask yourself the following questions:

   ~ *When I hear the word witch, how do I feel?*

   ~ *How do I feel now if different and why?*

   ~ *Am I worried about what others think if I call myself a witch?*

   ~ *Am I afraid of living openly as a witch?*

4. Now is a good time to light some incense.

5. On a piece of paper, I would like you to complete these statements:

   ~ *I don't feel validated because _____.*

~ *The following needs haven't been met:* _____.

~ *I'm scared of* _____ *because it makes me feel like* _____.

6. Now answer or reflect on the following questions and statements:

~ *What is one thing you've learned from thinking about the word witch and what it means to you?*

~ *Name and write about someone you've never met, but who has helped your life in some way.*

~ *How is your life more positive today than it was a year ago?*

7. Fold the piece of paper. Now say out loud:

> *I release that which is not mine. I release the energies that I am holding that no longer serve me. I release all obstacles on my path that do not bring me to my higher good. I release limiting beliefs, self-doubt and fear.*

8. Holding the folded paper in your hands, bring your hands to your heart space and say:

> *I call my power back to me, from every person, place, entity, space, portal, time and dimension. I am complete. What I am seeking is on its way to me. SO IT IS.*

9. Offer the paper to the candle flame allowing the fire to activate this energy. Place it straight into your fireproof container.

10. Once you've finished, return the cooled ashes to the Earth – sprinkle them outside in your garden or in your pot plants in your home.

The Importance of a Sisterhood

When embracing the witch within, it's also important to find a space where women support one another and hold space for each other without judgement. Find your tribe – a true circle of women who celebrate each other and hold no judgement of one another. Create a 'sisterhood'.

A sisterhood is a bond between women that transcends blood relations and is based on mutual love, support and understanding. It provides a sense of belonging, security and empowerment to women. Sisterhood also allows women to share their experiences, struggles and triumphs with each other without fear of judgement or rejection.

The importance of sisterhood can be seen in various aspects of life, such as personal growth, career development and social activism. Sisterhood plays a crucial role in the latter as it brings together like-minded women who work towards creating positive change in society. Women's movements throughout history have been successful because of the solidarity among women who fought for their rights. Women who have strong bonds with other women are also more likely to succeed in their personal and professional lives as they have a support system that encourages them to pursue their goals.

I hold space within sisterhood women's circles to inspire other women to create a sisterhood for themselves. I feel that it is essential for women to support each other through thick and thin as they navigate the challenges of life together. Try searching on social media to join groups of like-minded women or create your own women's circle event to make a sisterhood. Reach out and manifest your tribe to come forward. Try journaling around the question 'What does a sisterhood mean to me?' and call them forward. You can write this in the present tense and burn the piece of paper to release it to the universe.

Being a Witch Is a Part of You

When I started to trust that whisper of becoming the witch, I began to view the world differently, and so will you as you start to return home to yourself. I began to see situations with a dimensional lens, which helped me understand the world on a deeper and magical level. Over the years, throughout this journey, I have worked hard on myself. I have learned how to manage my stress and to heal and let go of my traumas – and, as a result, I reconnected to nature. This path showed me that my magic was held inside of me. It has made me more aware of my psychic abilities and intuition, and the natural energies of the world. It has given me a road to follow to return home to myself, which was always there; I just didn't know it.

I feel strongly that no one should tell you that you are doing it wrong or put across their point of view to discourage you from becoming a witch. If you feel as though you are a witch, then you are one; if you want to label yourself as a witch, you can. There is no right or wrong – this is YOUR journey.

When you feel ready, you can call yourself a witch.

True power comes from within – magic is in us all!

I do understand that, when you first start on this path as a witch, it can feel overwhelming. There is so much information out there, with so many rules! So where do you begin? From my experience, I would suggest connecting to within and spending some time journaling, asking yourself some questions around what is leading you in this direction:

● Why do you feel this pull towards witchcraft?

● What is it in you that is calling you to this path?

● What is your why?

● What's missing from your life that becoming a witch might fulfil?

Give yourself the chance to explore your thoughts and feelings around these prompts.

I recommend researching as much as you possibly can: read, read and read some more. Every author will have their own perspective, so make notes in your journal about what appeals to you. Remember that all of your life experiences will be incorporated into your body of knowledge as well. So, learn all that you can and jot down anything that resonates with you – not because you have been shown a direction through social media, but because it resonates with your soul. The most important thing when you are building a witchcraft practice is that you feel truly fulfilled by it and that you are finding peace within yourself and a connection with the Earth, to the universe and your spirituality.

I hope this chapter has helped you to see that you have what it takes to be a witch. You have started to uncover what that means for you and why you are drawn to the witch within – and you now understand why you may be fearful of taking this path so you can start to heal the witch wound. Now that you have this new sense of awareness, you can break free from the chains of oppression that have been placed upon women for centuries and really embrace your inner witch.

You're ready now to explore the fundamentals of witchcraft, which we'll cover in the next chapter.

CHAPTER 2

The Fundamentals
for the Witch

In order to fully embrace the path of a witch, it is crucial to understand and incorporate certain terms and practices into your daily life. These will serve as the building blocks of your journey and guide you back to your true self. By familiarizing yourself with these fundamental concepts, you can embark on a transformative journey towards becoming an empowered witch who is in tune with themselves and their surroundings.

The first practice I want to explore is 'grounding', which involves connecting with the Earth's energy to find stability and balance within yourself.

GROUNDING

Throughout this book I will often refer to grounding, which is when you connect to yourself with breathwork.

Here is my 'how-to' guide to grounding:

1. Take a few deep breaths.

2. Imagine that there's a white cord of energy extending from the base of your spine and connecting with the Earth. Imagine this energy flowing down into the roots of the Earth.

3. As you breathe inwards, pull up the energy from the Earth into your body, up to your heart space.

4. Exhale any energies within that are no longer yours down that cord and back into the Earth.

5. Do this for as long as you need to, until you feel grounded and connected.

Grounding your energy comes first, before you engage in anything. It will help you centre yourself amidst the chaos or when experiencing overwhelming emotions. When grounding, you want to be fully in your body, connected to your internal energy centres, to be able to connect to the dimensions around you, and regain balance and find calmness within.

You can also ground while out in nature by standing barefoot on the Earth and connecting to your breath. This physical contact with nature can rejuvenate your energy levels while simultaneously releasing any negative or stagnant energies accumulated within you.

Lastly, grounding facilitates a deeper connection for you by establishing a solid link between your energy field and higher realms of consciousness to the other dimensions. This heightened connection enables clearer communication during divination practices or when seeking guidance from dimensions (*we'll explore this fully in Part IV*).

Intentions

Being a witch is about harnessing your own power and using it alongside the power of the universe to manifest a life that aligns with your authentic self. The intention that you place is the direction in which this energy needs to flow.

Intention forms the core of any spell or ritual (we'll explore spells and rituals more deeply next). When crafting a spell or performing a ritual, you must first identify your intention. This could be anything from attracting love or wealth into your life, to seeking protection or healing. The more specific the intention, the more effective the spell or ritual becomes. The intention is the driving force behind the actions taken and the energy channelled. When you set an intention, your desire is clearly communicated by telling the universe what you want. Without a clear intention, spells and rituals lose their potency and become mere empty gestures. Intention provides focus, purpose and direction to these practices.

Clarity in intention allows you to align your thoughts, emotions and actions towards a common goal. Setting accurate intentions is a crucial aspect of casting spells and performing rituals effectively. Furthermore, spells and rituals are deeply intertwined with intention because they tap into the power of belief and faith. Belief acts as a catalyst for manifestation – it fuels our intentions and aligns us with the energy required to bring them to fruition. Without belief in the efficacy of spells or rituals, their impact diminishes significantly.

HOW TO SET INTENTIONS

To ensure that your intentions are clear and precise, follow these step-by-step instructions:

1. First, find a quiet and peaceful space where you can focus without any distractions. This will allow you to connect with your inner self and channel your energy more effectively.

2. Next, take several deep breaths to centre yourself and clear your mind of any clutter or negative thoughts. As you inhale, imagine drawing in positive energy and, as you exhale, release any tension or doubt that may be lingering within you.

3. Once you have attained a state of calm, it is time to formulate your intention. Begin by asking yourself what it is that you truly desire from the spell or ritual. Be specific in your desires; vague intentions may lead to unclear results. For example, instead of simply wishing for 'happiness', specify the aspects of your life in which you seek happiness – relationships, career, health, and so on – and envision how these areas will manifest positively.

4. Your intention is where most of the spell's or ritual's power will come from. Once you have that intention in your mind, you can harness that power by making sure all your thoughts and feelings support that intention. An intention involves determining your desired outcome from the spell or ritual, essentially defining what you seek to achieve through your magic.

5. After identifying your specific intention, write it down. This written representation will serve as a visual reminder throughout the casting process.

6. Now comes the moment to infuse your intention with energy. Hold the paper containing your written intention between both hands towards your heart space and close your eyes. Visualize the desired outcome vividly in your mind's eye while simultaneously feeling the emotions associated with achieving this outcome – joy, fulfilment and contentment.

+ ·,+ ✳· .+ .✴. + .✳.+·. +

Spells and Rituals

Once your intention is set, spells are often used as tools to manifest that desire into reality. Spells can take various forms – spoken incantations, written affirmations or even physical objects, such as candles or crystals charged with specific energies. These tools serve as conduits for focusing your energy towards achieving your intention. For example, you may harness the power of plants and herbs to amplify the effectiveness of your spells, given that each herb resonates with its own unique vibration (*see overpage*). Delve into the energies of each plant and herb, understanding their magic and traditional uses. Explore their correspondences with different intentions and energies, allowing your knowledge to deepen your magical work.

Using Plants and Herbs for Spells

Love and Romance

● Rose petals: for love, passion and romantic intentions.

● Lavender: promotes harmony, peace and attraction.

● Jasmine: enhances sensuality; fosters romantic connections.

Protection and Banishing

● Sage: clears negative energies; provides spiritual protection.

● Black salt: absorbs and repels negativity, creating barriers.

● Mugwort: shields against psychic attacks and negative influences.

Prosperity and Abundance

● Basil: attracts wealth, prosperity and abundance.

● Cinnamon: encourages success, luck and financial gain.

● Bay leaves: manifest wishes and bring opportunities for prosperity.

Healing and Wellness

● Chamomile: promotes relaxation, healing and emotional balance.

● Eucalyptus: clears energies, purifies spaces; aids in healing.

◑ Calendula: enhances physical healing and soothes emotional wounds.

Psychic Awareness and Intuition

◑ Mugwort: enhances psychic abilities and aids in divination.

◑ Blue lotus: stimulates intuition and enhances spiritual awareness.

◑ Patchouli: heightens psychic powers; strengthens intuition.

Creativity and Inspiration

◑ Lemon balm: boosts creativity, inspiration and mental clarity.

◑ Peppermint: stimulates the mind and enhances focus and creativity.

◑ Orange peel: invokes joy, creativity and enthusiasm.

Spirituality and Connection

◑ Frankincense: enhances spiritual connection and meditation.

◑ Myrrh: promotes introspection, spiritual growth and purification.

◑ Sandalwood: facilitates deep meditation and spiritual awakening.

Similarly, rituals provide structure and symbolism that reinforce your intentions. Rituals provide us with an opportunity to reconnect with ourselves on a deeper level. They serve as reminders to slow down and be present in the moment. By incorporating rituals into your daily routine, you create space for self-care and self-reflection. Rituals often involve repetitive actions performed in a specific order or sequence – such as lighting candles in a particular pattern or reciting prayers at designated times. These actions create a sense of rhythm and familiarity that helps you enter an altered state of consciousness conducive to manifestation.

When you perform a ritual with intention and focus, you will become more aware of your thoughts, feelings and surroundings. It provides a stillness, a pause in that present moment. An everyday act can become sacred by turning it into a ritual, whether it's drinking your cup of coffee in the morning in the garden, preparing food or taking a shower.

Other times for rituals include:

- The change of seasons: brings an opportunity for renewal and transition. See Chapter 4 for an exploration of the witch's Wheel of the Year.

- Cosmic events, such as a supermoon, eclipse or Mercury in retrograde: offers a powerful alignment for cosmic energies to be harnessed. See Chapter 5 for more on harnessing the wisdom of the moon.

- Something ending: marks a natural moment for closure and release.

- Something starting: signifies a fresh beginning and potential.

- Celebrating success or relationships: honours achievements and deepens connections.

◑ Clarity for an important decision or change: provides insight and guidance for pivotal moments in life.

The power of repetition lies in its ability to reprogram our subconscious mind – the seat of our beliefs and desires. By repeatedly performing rituals aligned with your intentions, you reinforce those desires on a subconscious level, making them more likely to manifest in your life.

Understanding the difference between a spell and a ritual is an important aspect of becoming an empowered witch. While spells are focused on manifesting specific outcomes using incantations or objects, rituals are more symbolic in nature and often involve repetitive actions that connect us with our higher selves or spiritual guides.

Cleansing

Another term I will use throughout the book is cleansing. Cleansing involves wafting smoke over the top of your head and your outer body (your aura) and also over your tools for the ritual or spell, and within the room/space that you are using. In some cultures, this is called 'smudging'. The cleansing tool you use can be your favourite incense sticks or cones, resin or dried plants that have been tied together to make a stick. I like to use 'a smoke wand'.

If you wish to make your own smoke wand, follow these simple guidelines:

1. Gather your ingredients. For a basic smoke wand, I use about four sprigs of rosemary and four sprigs of fresh garden sage (even better if you grow these herbs yourself in your garden).

2. Layer your ingredients, positioning the bases of the largest leaves at the same level as one another.

3. Cut a piece of cotton string and make a simple loose knot on one end of the string. Put the stems inside the knot, tighten it and bind the bundle together.

4. Begin to wrap the bundle tightly, spiralling up towards the top of the bundle. Fold in any stray sprigs, tucking them under the string as you go. Continue wrapping, crisscrossing the twine as you head back down towards the base. Tie the loose end to the original knot at the base of the stems.

5. Hang your smoke wand upside down in a sunny spot to dry for about three weeks before using.

Note: White sage is a herb sacred to Indigenous cultures and is currently being overharvested where it grows. Please therefore opt for garden sage or rosemary, mugwort, lavender or cedar instead.

HOW TO SMOKE-CLEANSE

If you are using a smoke wand, light one end with a match, blow out the flame and let the end continue to burn. You can fan the smoke with a feather or your hand. It is good to hold a bowl or shell underneath the wand to catch any embers. Your wand may go out a lot, so don't worry if you have to relight it. You can also place the wand into a fireproof bowl or shell while it is burning.

When you are finished, you can place the smoke wand in a fireproof bowl away from anything flammable and allow it to slowly burn itself out or run it under cold water and allow the herbs to dry out before using it again.

If you are using incense resin, this is usually used with a charcoal disc. Once the disc has been lit, wait for the outer edges to go white and then sprinkle the resin on top. This will produce a lot of smoke, so you might want to open your windows. I recommend frankincense resin as it smells divine, and it is a great protection smoke.

You can cleanse yourself or your home whenever you feel you want to. There is no right or wrong way. When you move around your room or home, it is good to hold an intention in your mind while you are cleansing. As you walk around, visualize the old, stagnant energy dissolving and fresh energy taking its place.

+ ˙ ,⁺ ✳ ˙ . ⁺ ˙ ✳ ˙ . ⁺ ˙ .⁺ ₊ ⁺ ˙ ⁺

Protection

Protection is an integral part of witchcraft as it involves safeguarding one's energy and connection to the divine. Protection from negative energies, entities or spirits can be achieved through rituals, spells or the use of protective amulets. By establishing a strong spiritual foundation, you can shield yourself from negative energies or psychic attacks that may be directed towards you.

Not everything that could negatively affect us comes from outside. We also need to protect ourselves from our own egos, doubts and fears, so protection spells can also be cast to protect ourselves from our own negative thoughts and feelings.

My father taught me the following white light protection spell, which you might like to try too:

WHITE LIGHT PROTECTION SPELL

1. Imagine yourself, or whatever else you want to protect, inside a bubble of protective white light. Nothing harmful can penetrate this white light.

2. Repeat the words:

   I am fully protected; I am safe.

3. Do this as many times as you need until you feel calm, safe and protected.

You can also create a protective barrier between the physical world and the spiritual realm by casting a circle.

HOW TO CAST A CIRCLE

1. Start by cleansing the area where you plan to cast your circle. This can be done through smoke cleansing or burning incense. The purpose of this step is to remove any negative energies or entities that may interfere with the ritual.

2. Now you can physically mark out the circle. Traditionally, this is done using salt or chalk to create a boundary on the ground. Alternatively, you can use string, ribbon, candles, lights or whatever you feel is right for you. The circular shape represents eternity and unity, and symbolizes the connection between all elements of nature.

3. After marking out the circle, you then call upon the four cardinal directions – north, south, east and west – as well as any deities or spirits you wish to invoke. Each direction holds its own significance: north represents stability and grounding; south embodies passion and transformation; east symbolizes new beginnings and inspiration; while west signifies emotions and intuition. State out loud your directions.

4. Next comes raising energy within the circle. You can do this through chanting or dancing in a clockwise direction around your sacred space.

5. Once enough energy has been raised, you then focus on setting your intentions for whatever ritual or spell you are performing within the circle. This could be anything from healing to manifestation or divination. The concentrated energy within the circle amplifies these intentions and sends them out into the universe.

6. Finally, when you have completed your work within the circle, it is important to close it properly. This involves thanking any deities or spirits that were invoked, releasing any remaining energy and physically dismantling the circle. This ensures that the sacred space is properly closed and that any residual energy is returned to its source.

+ · + ✦ · + ·☀· · + · ✦ + · · +

Overall, the benefits derived from grounding techniques, protection rituals and cleansing practices greatly contribute to your overall wellbeing. By incorporating these practices into your daily routine or spell work, you can harness their true potential while maintaining a harmonious connection with nature's forces. As you delve deeper into these aspects of witchcraft, you will undoubtedly find solace in knowing you possess the tools necessary to navigate through life's challenges confidently while embracing the magic within yourself.

*Being a witch is far more than
doing spells and rituals.*

Intuition

The witch wound, which we explored in the last chapter, has long
stifled our innate wisdom and connection to the unseen. As we
strive to reclaim our power, embrace our true selves and break
free from societal constraints, we can tap into the wellspring of
intuition that resides within us, guiding us towards authenticity,
empowerment and a more harmonious existence.

Every single one of us has been born with the intuitive gift of
'knowing' without intellectually understanding what is right for
us. Your subconscious mind is the source of your hidden genius
and will always provide you with the knowledge you need to move
forward in the right direction. This is true for all people, not just
those who consider themselves to be psychic.

Intuition, often referred to as a 'gut feeling', holds a profound
connection to our physical body. The notion of the gut being
the source of intuition is not merely metaphorical; it is rooted in
scientific understanding. Nestled within our solar plexus and third
chakra, just above the belly button, lies our gut – the epicentre of
intuitive sensations.

Gut feelings, also known as hunches or instincts, are those subtle
sensations that arise within us without any apparent logical basis.
They manifest as an intuitive sense of certainty or unease about a
particular situation or person. Often regarded as unexplainable,
gut feelings guide you towards making important decisions swiftly,
even when faced with limited information. These instinctual

reactions, often difficult to explain or dissect, possess a certain 'burstiness' that defies logical reasoning. In moments of uncertainty or imminent danger, our primal instincts kick in, propelling us to make split-second decisions that can sometimes defy conventional wisdom. It is in these instances of perplexity that intuition reveals its true power.

Our gut feelings are not limited to life-or-death situations, but also extend into various aspects of daily life. Consider those instances when you meet someone new and instantly form an impression about their character. This intuitive judgement occurs without any substantial evidence or logical reasoning; instead, it relies solely on the inexplicable signals transmitted by your subconscious mind – a manifestation of burstiness within you. Although we might not be able to articulate why we feel a certain way about someone upon first meeting them, there is an inherent trustworthiness in these snap judgements that should not be ignored.

The Power of the Present Moment

To help connect to your intuition, the biggest tip I can give you is to find time daily to be in the present moment. Being fully present is when we make time to stop, be still and pause to be fully aware of our thoughts, feelings and sensations without judgement or attachment. This pause encourages us to slow down and savour each moment as it unfolds, rather than constantly rushing towards the next task or goal.

Taking a deep breath is a simple yet powerful act that can help us reconnect with our bodies and bring awareness to the present moment. It serves as a reminder to slow down, let go of distractions and tune into our physical and emotional needs. By making conscious breathing a regular practice, you can create space for fresh energy and nourishment to flow into your being. This revitalizes both body and mind, allowing you to approach life with greater clarity and vitality.

Start now by taking that deep breath into your belly. Feel the expansion as you inhale deeply, then gently contract your navel towards your spine on the exhale. Notice how this simple act brings you back into your body and anchors you in the present moment.

By incorporating moments of pause to be in the present moment into your daily life, you can break free from the chains of constant distraction and find inner peace amidst chaos. When you do this, you become more attuned to your own needs and desires, allowing you to make choices that align with your values and bring you closer to a sense of fulfilment. This heightened self-awareness also extends to your relationships with others – when you are fully present in conversations or interactions, you deepen your connections and foster a greater understanding between yourself and those around you.

By carving out moments throughout your day for mindful practices such as meditation or deep breathing exercises, you can significantly enhance your ability to be fully present and connect to your intuition. These pauses also provide an opportunity for reflection and rejuvenation amidst life's constant whirlwind.

Meditation

You'll come to see that I mention meditation a lot throughout this book. It serves as an invaluable tool for quietening the mind, cultivating a deep sense of self-awareness and opening oneself up to higher frequencies. By sitting in stillness and silence, you can connect with your higher self and access the vast reservoirs of power within you.

Our minds are constantly racing, making it difficult to truly experience and appreciate the present moment and access those gut feelings I talked about above. Through regular meditation practice you can learn to detach from the constant stream of thoughts and emotions that often cloud your perception, and focus your attention inwards by calming your mind chatter. Meditation encourages you to observe your thoughts and emotions without judgement.

Furthermore, meditation helps us detach from negative emotions associated with past events or worries about future outcomes. By focusing on the present moment during meditation, we learn not to dwell on what has already happened or what might happen next. Instead, we train ourselves to accept things as they are in each passing moment.

To begin a meditation practice, find a quiet space where you will not be disturbed. Have your pen and journal ready nearby. Sit comfortably with your spine straight and close your eyes. Take several deep breaths, allowing yourself to relax and let go of any tension or stress.

As thoughts arise during meditation – which they inevitably will – gently acknowledge them without judgement or attachment, then let them go. Return your focus back to your breath and intention. Once you feel centred and calm, bring your attention to your intention or question. Clearly state it in your mind or out loud, allowing it to resonate within you.

As you continue meditating, focus on your breath as an anchor for your attention. With each inhale and exhale, imagine yourself becoming more open and receptive to the energies around you. Visualize yourself surrounded by a warm light that protects and guides you on this journey. I like to visualize a white door in my mind and, when I am ready, I open this door and step into a different reality, a different world, a higher dimension. I then begin to walk around this environment taking in everything I feel and see.

As you sit in silence and focus on your breath or a specific object, you may become aware of how easily your thoughts wander. Through consistent practice, you will learn to gently bring your attention back to the present moment whenever you notice yourself drifting away.

When your practice is done, just open your eyes and write in your journal all about your experience.

I truly believe that meditation saved my life and is my biggest medicine. It is my one non-negotiable that I will always do daily.

Mindfulness

Mindfulness involves paying attention intentionally and non-judgementally to what is happening in the present moment. By practising mindfulness during meditation, you develop an awareness of your thoughts, feelings, bodily sensations and surroundings without getting caught up in them. This helps you to understand yourself better and develop a deeper connection with others.

Journaling is also an excellent mindfulness practice that enables you to explore your thoughts, feelings and beliefs. It allows you to reflect on your experiences and gain insight into your own personal growth. I've included some journal prompts throughout the book to help you with this.

Visualization

Visualization is a powerful tool in many spiritual practices, including witchcraft, for manifesting desires and connecting with inner wisdom. To start, find a quiet and comfortable space where you won't be disturbed. Close your eyes, take some deep breaths and relax your body and mind. Begin by visualizing simple scenes or objects, focusing on details such as colours, textures and sensations. As you become more comfortable, progress to visualizing specific intentions or goals with clarity and vividness, engaging all your senses. Practise visualization regularly, ideally daily or several times a week, to strengthen your abilities and enhance your manifestation efforts. Remember, consistency and belief in the process are key to effective visualization.

The more time you spend with your soul through meditation, mindfulness and visualization, the clearer your intuition will become. When you are in alignment with who you are at the soul level and start to listen to your intuition, you will be in alignment with the rest of the universe.

10 Things I Wish I'd Known When I Started Witchcraft

1. Wearing black isn't necessary.

2. Covens aren't required.

3. There is nothing satanic in witchcraft.

4. A woman, man, or any other gender identity, may call themselves a witch.

5. Casting spells does not require you to use rare and weird materials, like in the movies. In fact, you need NOTHING but yourself to cast a spell.

6. Your magical journey is uniquely yours; there is no one-size-fits-all approach.

7. Embracing nature doesn't mean living in the woods – urban witches are just as connected.

8. Patience is a virtue; magical results may not be instant, and that's okay.

9. Learning and growing are continuous aspects of your witchcraft journey; it's a lifelong process.

10. There is no 'right' way to be a witch; find what resonates with you and embrace your own path.

On this journey of returning home to yourself, let's now explore the tools of the witch and how to set up the witch's sacred space – the altar.

CHAPTER 3

The Tools of the Witch

So many people ask me about the costs of becoming a witch, and I know there is a lot of talk online that to be a witch you need certain tools. As you will come to see, though, everything you actually need is within you and around you – for free!

I truly feel that the most powerful tools are from nature – they are in YOU: your intentions, energy, true will and light. You are always the most important part of any ritual or magical working. Without you, there is no magic.

However, throughout history, witches have used a variety of tools to enhance their magical practices, and we'll explore below those I suggest using in the rituals and spells in this book. These tools hold immense significance as they serve as an extension of oneself and a conduit for personal energy. They possess both symbolic and practical qualities, allowing us to invoke and welcome deities and harness the energies of the elements during magical work. Furthermore, these tools act as protective barriers against unwanted energies that may intrude upon our sacred space during a magical ritual. They are not meant to be seen as mere props or symbols, but rather as conduits for channeling your energy and intentions.

In this chapter, I will also guide you through the process of setting up a witch's sacred space. By creating a personalized altar, you can enhance your connection with the spiritual realm and harness its energy for spell work and rituals.

The Witch's Most Powerful Tools

- **Bowl:** an offering bowl, or container, is used to place offerings for your deities.

- **Broom:** the broom is the union of the female and male symbols of brush and staff, and as such was traditionally used in fertility ceremonies, festivals and rituals. The broom is usually made from straw, bound together at the end of a long wooden pole. It is used to spiritually cleanse and sweep negative energy from a space, purifying it before a ritual or spell work. I also use the broom as part of initiation rituals, showing how the new witch is crossing over into the circle and starting her path as a witch. We'll use the broom in your own initiation into becoming a witch in Chapter 16.

- **Candles:** these are used for many purposes, such as summoning deities or manifestation, and represent the fire element in spells and rituals. In my opinion, any candles can be used, though I would suggest using unscented ones if you wish to amplify the energy of the spell by adding herbs or essential oils. White is the purest form, so white dinner candles, tea light candles or pillar candles are ideal – you can even use birthday cake candles for fast spells!

◗ **Cauldron:** I use my cauldron in many ways, such as to burn incense and herbs, make offerings, or brew potions. A traditional three-legged witch's cauldron is made from cast iron. However, a cauldron can take the form of a saucepan or casserole dish, as long as it is capable of withstanding heat. You can use any fireproof container.

◗ **Crystals:** crystals hold the energy of the Earth and each one holds a unique vibrational frequency. I use them during meditation, manifestation and for spell work by choosing a crystal with an appropriate correspondence (*see below*).

Crystal Correspondences

These correspondences can vary slightly based on personal intuition, tradition and cultural associations. It's essential to choose crystals that resonate with you and your intentions.

~ **Amethyst:** promotes intuition, spiritual growth and inner peace; also used for protection.

~ **Aventurine:** attracts luck, prosperity and opportunities for growth; also supports heart healing.

~ **Black tourmaline:** provides protection against negativity, electromagnetic radiation and psychic attacks.

~ **Citrine:** encourages abundance, prosperity and manifestation of goals and desires.

~ **Clear quartz:** amplifies energy, enhances clarity and can be programmed for various purposes.

~ **Hematite:** grounds energy, enhances focus and provides protection; also used for manifestation.

~ **Labradorite:** enhances psychic abilities, intuition, and spiritual transformation.

~ **Moonstone:** enhances intuition and connection to lunar energies; aids in emotional balance.

~ **Obsidian:** shields against negativity, aids in grounding and facilitates shadow work.

~ **Rose quartz:** attracts love, fosters compassion and supports emotional healing.

~ **Selenite:** cleanses and charges other crystals, promotes mental clarity and connects to higher realms.

~ **Tiger's eye:** promotes courage, strength and protection; aids in decision-making and manifestation.

◐ **Cup/chalice:** the cup is variously used to hold the physical representation of water on the altar, as a receptacle or an offering, or as a vessel to share communion.

◐ **Incense:** I use incense to focus on my intentions for manifestation and meditate on my goals while it burns. I also work with incense for cleansing and blessing a space and purifying myself before casting a magic circle.

◐ **Knife/athame:** the knife is a symbol of fire, associated with action, decisiveness, resolve and confidence. It is used to direct energy, cast a circle or as an alternative to a wand. It is also used to carve symbols onto candles for spells.

Divination Tools

Some witches also like to use the following divination tools in their practice to receive messages and guidance, confirm their intuition and communicate with their guides:

● **Crystal balls:** these are used for scrying, a method of seeking insights and glimpses into the future or the unseen. Their smooth, spherical surface is believed to act as a portal for accessing higher realms or intuitive wisdom. You gaze into the crystal ball, allowing your mind to enter a trance-like state, where symbols, images or impressions may appear, guiding interpretation and offering guidance.

● **Dowsing rods:** these are utilized to detect energy fields or locate objects underground by responding to subtle shifts in electromagnetic or spiritual energies.

● **Oracle cards:** these offer guidance, insight and inspiration across various aspects of life. Each card is adorned with symbolic imagery and messages, allowing you to tap into intuition and higher wisdom. Through shuffling and drawing cards, seekers can receive answers to their questions or gain clarity on pressing issues, fostering personal growth and spiritual connection.

● **Pendulums:** pendulums are used for divination by interpreting the subtle movements in response to questions, providing clear yes or no answers or indicating directions for exploration.

● **Runes:** working with runes involves casting or drawing these ancient symbols carved onto stones or cards, interpreting their meanings and harnessing their energies for insight, guidance and divination.

● **Scrying mirrors:** working with scrying mirrors involves gazing into their reflective surface to access intuitive insights and spiritual guidance.

● **Tarot cards:** whether you're seeking clarity on decisions, exploring your inner self or are simply curious about the universe's whispers, tarot cards offer a pathway to insight and intuition. Let the cards illuminate your journey and awaken your spirit.

There are a few spells and rituals within the book that suggest using divination tools, but they are, of course, not essential.

Ultimately, what matters most is not the specific tools we possess, but rather how we use them in our magical practice: with intentionality, respect and reverence for the ancient craft of witchcraft.

And, of course, if you don't want to use any of these tools, that is okay. You don't need to do elaborate rituals or use a ton of ingredients for spell work. A simple candle surrounded by a few herbs from your kitchen will do just fine. Don't get hung up on what you feel you 'should' be doing in your magical practice; do what you feel intuitively and allow your magic to flow.

Everything you need is around or within you.

Creating an Altar

When you come to yourself as a witch, you must create a container to hold that power. That container is your altar. Your altar becomes a sacred space, a physical representation of your spiritual journey. It is where you connect with the divine forces that guide and empower you, and it is where you store your tools for making magic, if you choose to use them. As you step into your power as a witch, your altar will act as a vessel, holding the energy and intentions you channel.

When you approach your altar with reverence and intentionality, it becomes more than just an object; it becomes an extension of yourself. It is within this sacred space that true transformation occurs – where you embrace your power as a witch and manifest the life you deserve. My altar is my sacred space, a place where I do both my mundane and my most meaningful magic. It is a space where I can connect to all things and communicate with my higher self. As you grow into your journey of becoming a witch, your altar, too, can become a focal point for your rituals, spells and manifestations.

An altar can be anywhere in the home. It can live on a shelf, on top of a chest of drawers, on top of a box that you can pull out, on your dining table or in your garden – anywhere that is special for you. Altars are personal and they vary based on each person's own practice and path. There's no wrong way to create one – they can be minimalist or maximalist. So long as it is sacred to you, it is an altar. Building and maintaining an altar at home is a powerful way to cultivate a little sacred space in your everyday life.

To create your own altar, pick a space where you can focus your energy, your intentions and offer gratitude to the spirits, ancestors and energies that you work with. Decide on a set place in your home where you'll place your altar. It can be as big as a spare room or as small as a windowsill. It should be a space where you can connect to all things and communicate with your higher self. Altars can be created for a singular purpose, or multiple. You can have one altar and one altar only, or several. They can be dedicated to a deity, your ancestors, the elements or the seasons.

Use your intuition to collect any tools and objects that you would like to keep on your altar. What a witch chooses to put on their altar is personal, but below are some elements that you may like to consider adding to yours:

- Something that represents each element in its corresponding cardinal direction:
  - ~ Air: a found feather, a pen and paper, a smoke-cleansing wand.
  - ~ Fire: a candle in the colour related to your intention (*see opposite*).
  - ~ Water: a bowl or chalice of water.
  - ~ Earth: salt, a crystal, soil, seeds.

- **Candles:** these can serve as a representation of the element of fire and should be placed in the south area. As well as corresponding to your intention, candles can also be specific to the season, such as orange and yellow candles for the summer solstice. Candles are used in and as spells, and can be dressed in herbs, resins and oils, or placed on top of spell jars for sealing in intentions. When burning herbs, papers or bay leaves, I always use the flame from a candle to do so.

Candle Colour Meanings

Choose candle colours that resonate with your specific goals and intentions for effective candle magic. You will always find white and black candles on my altar for both protection and purification.

- ~ **Black:** banishing, protection, absorbing negativity, releasing.

- ~ **Blue:** peace, tranquillity, communication, truth, wisdom, protection.

- ~ **Brown:** grounding, stability, home, endurance, animal magic.

- ~ **Gold:** wealth, success, achievement, abundance, solar energy.

- ~ **Green:** abundance, prosperity, fertility, growth, healing, nature.

- ~ **Orange:** creativity, success, enthusiasm, attraction, encouragement.

- ~ **Pink:** romantic love, friendship, harmony, emotional healing.

- ~ **Purple:** Psychic abilities, intuition, spiritual power, ambition, wisdom.

- ~ **Red:** passion, love, courage, vitality, energy, strength.

- ~ **Silver:** intuition, dreams, psychic development, feminine energy.

~ **White:** purity, spiritual enlightenment, cleansing, protection.

~ **Yellow:** confidence, intellect, communication, clarity inspiration.

- **Cauldron:** to safely burn incense, herbs and paper for releasing or manifesting.

- **Chalice:** this can be a water element representation and should be placed in the west if that is the intention. It could also be used for wine, tea or honey offerings.

- **Crystals:** these can be an essential part of your altar, tapping into their energy to enhance your magical workings. Crystals don't have to be huge – a small, tumbled crystal will work well too. You can choose which crystal energy best works for the intentions of your altar (*see page 45*).

- **Divination tools:** these can be useful additions to your altar primarily because they facilitate communication with the different dimensions, provide guidance and deepen spiritual insights through divination practices (*see page 47*).

- **Natural and found objects:** things like shells, bones and feathers connect you to the natural world and its inherent energies.

- **Offerings:** these include gifts of food, drinks or flowers – or things that would be well received by the deity or deities you're working with, your ancestors, animal spirits or Mother Nature herself. You just need a dish or vessel of some kind to hold your offerings.

◑ **Photographs of your ancestors:** These enable you to link to your familial past, honouring the wisdom, guidance and legacy of your ancestors. This strengthens family bonds and offers spiritual guidance and protection.

◑ **Pictures, artwork or old photos:** Using your altar space to hold anything that is especially significant and personal to you is a great way to keep memories, pets or people close.

◑ **Statues and symbols:** These can be kept on your altar to honour or represent the deities. They can be useful because they serve as focal points for devotion and connection.

I like to change my altar during the different moon phases that I am working with (*see Chapter 5*), or seasonally, or to celebrate a Sabbath (*see Chapter 4*), or to connect to a different dimension (*see Chapter 14*). Cleaning and dressing the altar is something I love to do as it's a form of meditation and helps me focus my intentions while I am creating it.

When first creating your altar, I recommend starting small with something as simple as a single candle and a picture of someone who reminds you of what you'd like to cultivate more of in your life.

In addition to your primary working altar, you can also create altars to build power for specific intentions and projects. You can create altars for all kinds of intentions, such as a self-love altar in your bathroom or a cooking altar in your kitchen, or even one in your garden to honour the changes in the seasons.

An Example of an Altar Devoted to Self-Love and Care

- Crystal: choose rose quartz.

- Essential oils: choose oils like rose, lavender or jasmine for their calming and self-soothing properties.

- Mirror: symbolizes self-reflection and encourages introspection and self-awareness.

- Affirmation cards: write positive affirmations or quotes on small cards to reinforce self-love and confidence.

- Statues or figurines: include representations of deities or symbols associated with self-love, such as the goddesses Venus or Aphrodite.

- Journal and a pen: provide a space for reflection and writing down your thoughts, feelings and intentions related to self-love and care.

- Shells: representing purification and rejuvenation, these are perfect for self-care rituals like baths or cleansing ceremonies.

- Personal mementos: add items that hold personal significance or bring you joy, such as photographs, trinkets or tokens of self-appreciation.

- Incense or a sage smoke wand: use for cleansing and purifying the space, creating a sacred atmosphere for self-love rituals.

- Offerings: consider offerings such as fruits, sweets or drinks that nourish and delight your senses, symbolizing love and appreciation.

Looking back on my path of returning to the witch I am today, it has been about trusting myself and the universe, working with my soul, mind, body, the Earth, the universe and the dimensions. By embracing my beliefs and fears, and stepping into the unknown, I uncovered aspects of myself I never knew existed. I transformed the trauma from my past, balanced my nervous system and alchemized my energetics. It is my hope that you, too, will experience these benefits. In Part II, you'll take one step closer by learning about the magic from the natural world.

PART II

Uncovering Magic from the Natural World

One of the biggest tools that has guided my life is living in sync with the rhythms and energies of nature, following the cycles of the seasons and adapting to the changes that occur throughout the year. I believe that in life we sometimes need help from the world and universe around us, from the fungi, flowers and plants, to the bees, animals, trees and seasons. Cultivating a profound and unbreakable bond with the natural world is an essential aspect of embracing your inner witch – this connection has served as a vital source of power, wisdom and inspiration for witches throughout history.

In this section of your journey, we'll therefore delve into the enchanting realm of the natural world, where magic thrives in every corner, uncovering the intricate web of life surrounding you and how it can provide guidance, healing and wisdom.

The Earth and the universe serve as essential allies of spiritual growth and magical practices. The Earth provides energy through its elements, while the moon guides emotional cycles and stellar connections offer insights.

You will learn to harness the power of plants, their healing properties and mystical energies that connect us to ancient wisdom. And let us not forget the animals who share their profound insights with us, guiding our intuition and awakening our primal instincts.

This is an important dimension to teach you because I feel that, in today's world, where many of us are disconnected from nature's wonders, exploring the relationship between yourself and your environment can remind you of your interconnectedness with the universe at large. By embracing this connection, you may find inspiration in aligning yourself with natural forces that can enhance your own wellbeing and spiritual growth. This way of living will bring you closer to nature, help you to feel more connected to the environment and improve your overall wellbeing.

Drawing power from the Earth, moon, stars and other celestial bodies, and the universe, will support you on your way home to yourself and facilitate your life by providing you with guidance, energy and a sense of belonging. Embracing this magic from nature is a vital step towards unlocking your own inner power as a witch.

CHAPTER 4

The Witch's Calendar

The Earth, with her ever-changing seasons, unveils a tapestry of wonders that teach us about growth, transformation and resilience. In this chapter, we'll look at how to honour the cycles of nature and the changing seasons.

The Wheel of the Year

The witch's Wheel of the Year is a powerful tool for connecting with nature, celebrating life's cycles and deepening one's spiritual practice. It is a sacred calendar that marks the eight seasonal festivals celebrated by Wiccans and other pagan traditions. These festivals are known as 'Sabbaths' and are divided into two solstices, two equinoxes and four cross-quarter days. Each Sabbath has its own unique symbolism and rituals. By honouring these Sabbaths, you can connect with nature's cycles and find balance within yourself.

Solstices

Solstices are celestial events that mark the longest and shortest days of the year. Solstices occur twice a year, once in June and again in December. The summer solstice, known as Litha, marks the longest day of the year when the sun reaches its highest point in the sky. It falls on around 21 June in the northern hemisphere and around 21 December in the southern hemisphere. The winter solstice, known as Yule, marks the shortest day of the year when the sun reaches its lowest point in the sky. It falls on around 21 December in the northern hemisphere and around 21 June in the southern hemisphere. (The dates vary by a day or two depending on the year and the location.)

Solstices have been celebrated by various cultures throughout history as they mark significant changes in nature and are often associated with rebirth and renewal. Litha encourages us to bask in the sun's warmth and embrace our inner light, fostering confidence and self-expression, while Yule marks the rebirth of the sun, inspiring renewal and goal-setting, encouraging us to envision and manifest our aspirations.

In ancient times, people would gather at Stonehenge in Wiltshire, England, to witness the sunrise on summer solstice. Similarly, many Native American tribes celebrate solstices with rituals and ceremonies. Today, solstices continue to be celebrated around the world through various cultural traditions, such as lighting bonfires or lanterns to symbolize light overcoming darkness. Solstices remind us of our connection to nature and offer an opportunity for reflection and renewal as we move through each season.

Equinoxes

Equinoxes are the two points in the year when day and night are of equal length. These events occur twice a year: the vernal or spring equinox, which occurs around 20 March in the northern hemisphere and 22 September in the southern hemisphere; and the autumn equinox on around 22 September in the northern hemisphere and 20 March in the southern hemisphere. Again, these dates vary. The equinoxes mark the beginning of spring and autumn respectively and have been celebrated by many cultures throughout history. They represent a balance between light and dark, and life and death.

The spring equinox, known as Ostara, which is named after the Germanic goddess of spring, celebrates balance and abundance, prompting us to nurture our dreams and bring them to fruition. Mabon, the autumn equinox, emphasizes balance and harmony, guiding us to find equilibrium and wisdom in our lives.

Cross-quarter Days

The four remaining Sabbaths are known as cross-quarter days, marking important agricultural events in ancient times. Each festival has its own unique rituals and customs that reflect its significance:

◑ Imbolc falls around 1 February in the northern hemisphere and 1 August in the southern hemisphere. This heralds the awakening of spring, igniting creativity and passion within us as we honour the goddess Brigid and cultivate our talents.

◑ Beltane falls around 1 May in the northern hemisphere and 1 November in the southern hemisphere. This is all about the celebration of fertility and union, and fosters connections with nature and community, guiding us to explore our desires and relationships.

◑ Lammas falls around 1 August in the northern hemisphere and 1 February in the southern hemisphere. The first harvest, this invites reflection on abundance and gratitude, inspiring us to honour our achievements and share our blessings.

◑ Samhain falls around 31 October in the northern hemisphere and 1 May in the southern hemisphere. This invites introspection and connection with ancestral wisdom, empowering us to release the past and embrace our inner strength. It also encourages us to honour our ancestors and connect to the spirit world.

The Wheel of the Year serves as both a practical tool for marking time and a spiritual guide for personal growth and transformation. It also reminds us to live in harmony with nature, to appreciate its beauty and power, and to recognize our place within it. Each season has its own unique energy and rhythm, which we can tap into by adjusting our daily routines and activities. For example, during springtime when everything is blooming and coming back to life, we might feel more energized and motivated to start new projects or take on new challenges. In contrast, during winter when everything is dormant and quiet, we might feel more introspective and reflective.

*Move through the year by going
inwards, resting and then blooming,
rebirthing and celebrating.*

I would like to guide you now through the year as a witch, starting with autumn as, for me, I look at Samhain as my New Year's Eve.

Autumn

Autumn is the season for honouring, harvesting and divination. During autumn there is Samhain, which marks the end of the harvest season and the beginning of winter. At Samhain, the veil between the living and the dead is at its thinnest.

The Samhain ritual traditionally involved lighting bonfires, dressing up in costumes and offering food and drink to ancestors who had passed away. It was also a time for divination, where people would try to predict their future using various methods such as apple-bobbing or reading tea leaves. Many of these rituals still exist today. The significance of Samhain goes beyond just honouring our ancestors; it also represents a time for reflection and introspection. As we enter into winter, we are reminded of our mortality and encouraged to take stock of our lives. It serves as a reminder that, even in death, our loved ones are still with us in spirit.

SAMHAIN RITUAL

This is a ritual to honour your loved ones in the spirit world. It will help you with grief, so please be gentle with yourself during this time.

The perfect time for this ritual is: Samhain.

TOOLS

For this ritual you will need the following items:

-) tools for casting a circle (*see page 34*)
-) matches
-) candles, such as pillar, dinner, spells or tea light candles – you can use white or orange-coloured ones to reflect the season
-) nature's autumn treasures, such as pinecones, leaves and pumpkins
-) incense sticks or cones to burn
-) photographs of your loved ones in the spirit world
-) any mementos that represent your loved ones in the spirit world
-) a pen and two pieces of A4 paper
-) a cauldron or fireproof container

INSTRUCTIONS

1. To begin your Samhain ritual, create a sacred space by casting a circle. You can do this by visualizing a circle of white light around you or physically marking out a circle with candles or stones (*see page 34*). Once you have created your circle, call upon the elements to join you in your ritual. You can do this by lighting candles or incense to represent each element (Fire for south, Air for east, Water for west, Earth for north)

or simply calling out their names. Then decorate the space with your autumn treasures.

2. Next, take some time to honour your ancestors. You can do this by lighting candles or incense in their memory or creating an ancestor altar with pictures and mementos of those who have passed on. Take some time to reflect on their lives and how they have influenced yours. You may also wish to ask them for guidance or support in your life.

3. After honouring your ancestors, it's time to release what no longer serves you. This could be anything from negative thought patterns to toxic relationships or habits that are holding you back from reaching your full potential. Write down what you want to release on one piece of paper and then burn it in a cauldron or fireproof container as an act of letting go.

4. Once you have released what no longer serves you, it's time to set intentions for the coming year (*see page 26*). Think about what you want to manifest in your life and write it on the other piece of paper. You can also create a vision board or use visualization techniques to help bring your intentions to life.

5. To close your Samhain ritual, thank the elements for their presence and release the circle by visualizing the white light dissipating or physically extinguishing any candles that were used or removing the stones. Take some time to ground yourself by eating a nourishing meal or spending time in nature.

By honouring your ancestors, releasing what no longer serves you and setting intentions for the future, you can tap into the energy of this sacred season and create positive change in your life.

+ ˙ ₊ ✳ ˙ ₊ ˙ ✴ ˙₊ ˙ ✳ ₊˙ ₊

Winter

Winter is a time for reflection and hibernation, resting and healing. The winter solstice marks the longest night of the year, and it is during this time that you can come together with your friends or family to celebrate and honour the darkness.

WINTER SOLSTICE RITUAL

This ritual is a way for you to connect with nature and tap into its power as you prepare for the coming year. This ritual is perfect to do with family or friends as a group.

The perfect time for this ritual is: winter solstice.

TOOLS

For this ritual you will need the following items:

› matches

› candles, such as pillar, dinner, spells or tea light candles

› incense sticks or cones to burn

› tools for casting a circle (*see page 34*)

INSTRUCTIONS

1. Create a peaceful environment by dimming the lights and lighting candles within the room/space you are working in. You may also choose to burn incense such as pine, cinnamon or anything that gives you a festive feeling.

2. Sit around a table as a group.

3. To begin your winter solstice ritual, start by casting a circle (*see page 34*).

4. Call on the elements by saying:

> *Guardians of the Watchtowers,*
> *I call upon you the powers of Earth, Air, Fire and Water*
> *to protect and consecrate this circle.*
> *What is above will be so below.*
> *I call on you to bless this circle,*
> *free from negativity and harm.*
> *This circle is cast, safe and secure.*
> *So mote it be!*

5. To close, say:

> *Guardians of the Watchtowers,*
> *I thank you for your presence and power here tonight,*
> *north, east, south and west.*
> *My rites here are done.*
> *By the power of the moon.*
> *By the light of the sun.*
> *So mote it be!*

6. Once you have released the circle, sit comfortably with closed eyes and visualize the energy you have raised as a ball of pure white light.

7. Now, meditate on your intentions for the coming year, reflecting on what you want to achieve in your personal life as well as in your spiritual practice. This reflection will help you to set goals and intentions that will guide you throughout the year ahead.

8. After meditating on your intentions, it is nice to share them openly within the group. Then it is great to have a feast together or sit around an open fire to talk and celebrate the year that is ending and the new year that is coming.

Spring

Spring is a time when the Earth awakens from its winter slumber and begins to bloom once again. The spring equinox is a time of renewal, rebirth and growth. For witches, this is a time of celebration and ritual. The spring equinox marks the halfway point between the winter solstice and the summer solstice.

SPRING JOURNAL PROMPTS:

> What new beginnings are happening in your life right now? How do they make you feel?

> Take a walk outside and observe the changes happening in nature around you. Write about what you see and how it makes you feel.

> What are some things that make you feel refreshed and renewed? How can you incorporate them into your daily routine?

> Write about a time when you overcame an obstacle or challenge. What did you learn from this experience?

> What is something that scares you, but also excites you at the same time? Why does it have this effect on you?

Summer

Summer is the time to celebrate and see our manifestations come to life. Be surrounded by nature and enjoy the energy of the sun. During this season it is easy to feel overwhelmed and worn out, so self-love and self-care are at the top of the list for your own energy to be at its highest.

SUMMER SOLSTICE RITUAL

This ritual will help you see and feel ways in which you are stuck and holding yourself back. In order to manifest, we must make room for new energy to flow in, letting go of things that no longer serve us.

The perfect time for this ritual is: summer solstice or on a full moon.

TOOLS

For this ritual you will need the following items:

> a pen and a piece of A4 paper

> matches

> a cauldron or fireproof container

INSTRUCTIONS

1. Write down all the things that make you feel stuck. Be honest and clear, even if that is difficult or painful.

2. Reflect and meditate on your obstacles. Does your heart feel heavy? How much of what's holding you back is within your control? As you reflect, imagine these obstacles becoming smaller and more powerless.

3. Write down an intention to push back against these challenges, such as 'I am ready to release the people who hold me back.'

4. Light the paper on fire and drop it carefully into a cauldron or fireproof container.

5. Gather the cooled ashes and flush them away down a toilet or place them in your bin. You want to remove them from your space as you have let go of them.

+ · ,+ ✳ . + . ✳ . + · ✳ ,+ . +

By observing these ancient celebrations, you can connect with your spiritual roots and deepen your connection to nature. You can also use this time to set intentions for yourself and your community, casting spells for healing, abundance or protection. I celebrate the Sabbaths to honour life's natural rhythms and tap into the power of magic. It is a reminder that we are all connected to each other and to the Earth itself.

Another way you can live in sync with nature is by paying attention to the natural cycles of light and dark. Our bodies are designed to respond to these cycles, so it's important to get enough sunlight during the day and avoid bright screens at night. This means spending time outdoors during daylight hours and taking breaks from work to go for a walk or sit outside in nature.

You can also eat seasonal foods that are fresh and locally grown to honour the seasons. Eating foods that are in season not only supports local farmers, is more cost-effective and kind to the planet, but it also provides us with nutrients that are naturally available at different times of year. For example, during winter months we might eat more root vegetables like carrots or sweet potatoes, which provide warmth and nourishment for our bodies.

Exercise is another important aspect of living in sync with nature. During different seasons we may need different types of exercise depending on what feels good for our bodies at that time. In summer months it might be swimming or hiking, while winter months may call for indoor activities like yoga or Pilates. By listening to our bodies and adapting our exercise routines to the changing seasons, we can stay healthy and energized throughout the year.

In embracing the wisdom of the seasons, we come to understand that life is a cyclical journey. Just as the Earth experiences periods of growth and rest, so do we. The changing seasons remind us to find moments of stillness amidst the chaos, allowing us to recharge and reflect. During the winter months, when days are shorter and nights are longer, it's natural to feel more tired or sluggish. This is a good time to slow down, take naps or get extra sleep at night.

Nature's cycles also teach us the importance of celebration and honouring. We learn to acknowledge our achievements and milestones, just as we rejoice in the bountiful harvests of nature. Through this recognition, we cultivate gratitude and a deeper connection with ourselves and the world around us.

As well as being connected to the seasons, one of the biggest ways that I connect with nature is by working with the phases of the moon, which we'll explore in the next chapter.

CHAPTER 5

The Wisdom of the Moon

We are all connected to the cycles of the moon more than we realize. Not only does the moon impact our emotions, it also affects the world around us through the power of gravity and tidal pulls.

The moon plays an integral role in witchcraft practices due to its cyclical nature and association with feminine energy. For me, working with the moon gives me the opportunity to regularly check in with myself, set new intentions and validate my insights. It has also helped me be more intentional with where I choose to devote my energy in each cycle and how I approach my desires and goals. Every time a new cycle begins, the slate is wiped clean and I get a fresh start. No matter what happened before, it's a chance to start again.

In this chapter, I want to share with you how you, too, can work with the moon's magic. We'll explore how to harness the phases of the moon, as well as other energies you can tap into, such as lunar eclipses, supermoons and the star signs.

The Phases of the Moon

The moon, like women, moves in cycles through her phases. Each phase brings a different energy, a unique essence that captivates and influences the world around us. Just as the moon's energy and light waxes and wanes, so too do women's lives ebb and flow with their own inner rhythms.

The moon's energy and light waxes
and wanes, and so do we.

The eight lunar phases are:

1. New moon
2. Waxing crescent
3. First quarter/half-moon
4. Waxing gibbous
5. Full moon
6. Waning gibbous
7. Last quarter
8. Waning crescent

You can coordinate your rituals with any of these lunar phases, but, as life is busy and I am a modern witch, to help me to align to the natural world I work with the four main moon phases – new, waxing, full and waning – by doing a corresponding ritual to invoke its greatest power in each one. This means it doesn't feel overwhelming trying to work with each phase.

Let's now look at how you can do the same.

New Moon: Pause

The new moon represents new beginnings as we plant seeds for the month ahead. Then, for the next two weeks, it gradually builds in strength towards the full moon. On the new moon I sit in reflection with my journal and begin to feel into my body what intentions I want to set, clarify my goals, start new projects and acknowledge my growth since the previous new moon. New moon energy can be honoured the day before, the day of and the day after the actual new moon.

NEW MOON RITUAL

Light a candle and grab your journal. Date the top of the page along with the words 'New Moon Intentions'. Then, close your eyes for a few deep breaths and, when you are ready, write down three to five core intentions for this moon cycle, writing in the first person and present tense as though it's already happening. For example, 'My intentions for this new moon are to give myself some space for self-care, start my new creative project and set some strong boundaries.'

When you are done, read each one out loud, stating, 'And so it is' after each spoken intention. Some intentions may take a few moon cycles to fully materialize. Be grateful as your intentions come to life.

Below are some journal prompts that will help you during this new moon ritual:

) What does my heart truly desire?

) What is the truest, most beautiful life I can imagine for myself?

) What are three goals I want to accomplish this month?

) What boundaries am I setting to support my growth and wellbeing?

❭ Describe the dream life you want to create for yourself as if you already have it. Express true joy, awe and gratitude for how everything has worked out perfectly for you.

NEW MOON SPELL FOR MANIFESTATION

As the new moon is the ideal time during the month to feel into what we want to call into our lives, this is a great spell to do during this time. Really feel into what you would like to manifest into your life within the next month.

The perfect time for this spell is: new moon.

TOOLS

For this spell you will need the following items:

❭ matches

❭ a candle or some incense

❭ a pen and a piece of A4 paper

❭ your mobile phone or journal

INSTRUCTIONS

1. Find a quiet and peaceful space where you can connect with the energy of the new moon.

2. Light a candle or some incense to create an atmosphere of tranquillity.

3. Take a few deep breaths to ground yourself and clear your mind.

4. On a piece of paper, write down your intention or desire in clear and concise language. Be specific about what you want to manifest in your life.

For example, if you are seeking love, write down qualities you desire in a partner or specific actions you would like them to take. Write *why* you want this to come into your life.

5. Keep a note of what you want to call in by photographing this piece of paper or copying what you have written into your journal.

6. Fold the paper three times towards yourself while visualizing your desire coming true.

7. Hold it in your hands and visualize yourself already having achieved what you desire. Feel the emotions associated with this manifestation – joy, gratitude, excitement – as if it has already happened. The more vividly you can imagine this reality, the stronger the energy will be behind your spell.

8. Now it is time to release this energy into the universe. Bury the folded paper outside under the new moon. As you do so, say aloud:

    Under this new moon's energy, I release my intentions into flow.
    May they manifest with grace, bringing blessings to my space.

9. Leave the paper undisturbed until after sunrise the next day. At that time, retrieve the paper and, if it is still legible and intact, keep it in a safe place. This spell is all about seeing progress, and keeping track of what you have called into your life will help with that.

+ · + ✳ · + · ✳ · + · ✳ ·+ · +

Remember, casting spells is not about controlling or manipulating others; it is about aligning your energy with the universe's natural flow. The new moon provides a powerful opportunity to tap into this energy and manifest your desires. By performing this spell with pure intentions and an open heart, you are inviting positive change into your life.

Waxing Moon: Action

The waxing moon is when the light of the moon gradually begins to expand and grow in its fullness, serving as fuel during this phase. The waxing moon is a good time to get motivated, commit to what you are building and put your intentions into action. During this time, the energy of the moon is supporting you in nurturing the seeds you've planted for bringing new projects to life. It encourages you to take inspired, courageous and aligned action towards creating what it is you desire. This is a magnetic time for transformation, so this is when you can say yes to everything, network, launch new things and go, go, go.

Waxing Moon Ritual

During this phase, grab a pack of oracle cards for inspired action. Pause for a couple of deep breaths, tune into your intentions and shuffle the cards. Spread out the cards and hover your left hand over them until you feel a magnetic pull. Draw two cards. The first one brings clarity to your core intention and the second represents the support or action needed to nurture this intention. Sit with what arises as you contemplate your cards.

Below are some journal prompts that will help you during this waxing moon ritual:

> What steps do I need to take in order to achieve my desires?

> How are my intentions being blocked?

Full Moon: Celebration

The full moon is the phase when the sun illuminates the entire moon, making her as full, round and bright as can be. This phase represents completion, fertility, abundance and transformation, when the seeds from the new moon come into bloom. Because the moon is directly opposite the sun during this phase, it can also be a time of more intense emotional energy so performing spells during a full moon can enhance their potency. Plus, your intuition may be more awake, so listen closely to what you intuitively want to shed, let go of and release. For me, this is a time for reflection, to celebrate what I have achieved, give gratitude, clean and cleanse, do divination work, hold events and perform rituals if I feel called to do so. Full moon energy can be worked with on the day before, the day of and the day after the actual full moon.

Full Moon Celebration Ritual

As the full moon rises in the sky, you are presented with a potent opportunity for celebration and manifestation. The full moon's radiant energy illuminates the darkness, guiding you on a journey of introspection, release and renewal. This ritual is designed to harness the mystical energy of the full moon, allowing you to release what no longer serves you and set intentions for abundance and blessings to flow into your life. Gather your tools and prepare to embark on a sacred journey under the gentle, loving glow of the moon.

The perfect time for this ritual is: full moon.

TOOLS

For this ritual you will need the following items:

- ❭ a cleansing tool, such as incense, a smoke wand or resin
- ❭ matches
- ❭ a white candle
- ❭ a pen and a piece of A4 paper
- ❭ a cauldron or fireproof container
- ❭ an oracle deck (if you have one)
- ❭ your journal

INSTRUCTIONS

1. Start by smoke cleansing yourself and the space you are in.

2. Light your candle and open your space energetically by stating:

> *I call forward the element of Air.*
> *I call forward the element of Fire.*
> *I call forward the element of Earth.*
> *I call forward the element of Water.*

Then state the following:

> *Under the full moon's light*
> *I embrace its power, shining bright.*
> *In your gentle, loving glow*
> *may abundance and blessings flow.*
> *Moon Goddess, guide my way,*
> *illuminate my path today.*

3. Then, sitting comfortably, ground yourself so that you are plugged into the dimensions of the Earth and the universe (*see page 24*).

4. Close your eyes and begin to visualize your intentions, your manifestations and your desires. Ask your soul what's holding you back.

5. Open your eyes and, on the piece of paper, write what you are grateful for from the last four weeks.

6. Now, look at the things that are holding you back, the things that are blocking you. What do you want to let go of as they no longer serve you? Write these down like this: 'I let go of _____ as they no longer serve me.'

7. Lastly, write a list in the present tense of what you desire to call into your life. Like this: 'I call forward the following _____.'

8. Fold the paper towards you and, holding it in your palms towards your heart space, state to the flame the following:

    I release any negative energy or emotions that no longer serve me.
    I let go of any fears or doubts and trust in the divine plan for my life.
    I release any attachments to the past and welcome new beginnings.
    I am in perfect harmony with the universe and my dreams are
    coming to fruition. I know all I desire is already here. And so it is.

9. Now give thanks and offer your paper to the flame, dropping it into your cauldron or fireproof container safely as it burns under the full moon. Sprinkle the cooled ashes onto your outside space.

10. To close, you can shuffle an oracle deck and pull out three cards and journal how those cards relate to your ritual.

Waning Moon: Release

Waning refers to the decreasing of the moon's light, inviting us to surrender, renew, withdraw and rest. This is a good phase to reflect and contemplate on what is ending so you can prepare to plant new seeds or tend to those that need nurturing as the moon once again makes her way towards the new moon. The waning moon is also a time to declutter, cleanse, heal, end chapters and do banishing work, decluttering your social media, ready for the new cycle to begin again.

It feels amazing to walk into a clean and clear space in our homes, so, during this phase, try to release the clutter and create a sacred space to dwell in so that your mind and energy feel clear. This is also a good time to tend to your altar, cleaning it and reorganizing it to reflect your intentions. During the waning moon, I like to do a cleansing ritual, which I have shared with you below.

Waning Moon Cleansing Ritual

The waning moon offers a sacred opportunity for cleansing, renewal and connection with lunar energies. This ritual is designed to help you release negativity, recharge your spirit and align with the healing power of the moon. Prepare to immerse yourself in a nurturing bath experience that honours the natural rhythms of the lunar cycle.

The perfect time for this ritual is: waning moon.

Tools

For this ritual you will need the following items:

❭ matches

❭ white candles

❭ cleansing herbs such as sage, rosemary or lavender (optional)

❭ crystals (optional)

❭ Epsom salts or Himalayan pink salt

❭ lavender essential oil (or your preferred scent)

❭ smoke wand (optional)

❭ your favourite relaxing music or meditation guide (optional)

❭ a soft towel

INSTRUCTIONS

1. Begin by setting up your bathroom as a sacred space. Light white candles to create a soothing ambience.

2. If you have cleansing herbs or crystals, place them near the bathtub or around the room.

3. Fill your bathtub with warm water and add a generous amount of Epsom salts or Himalayan pink salt. These salts will help to detoxify your body and promote relaxation.

4. Add a few drops of essential oil to the water. Lavender is known for its calming and cleansing properties, and is perfect for a moon bath ritual.

5. If you have a smoke wand, light it and allow the smoke to purify the bathroom space. You can also use a smudging spray if preferred.

6. Before entering the bath, take a moment to set your intentions for the ritual. Visualize releasing any negative energy or emotions and inviting in peace, clarity and healing.

7. Step into the bathtub and immerse yourself in the warm water. Close your eyes and feel the healing energy of the moon enveloping you.

8. Take slow, deep breaths, allowing yourself to relax fully into the experience. Visualize any tension or negativity melting away with each exhale.

9. If desired, play your favourite relaxing music or meditation guide to deepen your connection with the lunar energy. Alternatively, simply enjoy the peaceful silence and solitude of the bath.

10. Take this time to reflect on any insights or guidance that may arise. Listen to your inner wisdom and trust in the messages from the moon.

11. As you soak in the bath, express gratitude for the cleansing and healing energy of the moon. Feel a sense of renewal and empowerment washing over you.

12. When you feel ready, slowly rise from the bath and wrap yourself in a soft towel. Take a moment to ground yourself and integrate the experience.

13. Blow out the candles and thank the moon for its blessings. Carry the sense of peace and purification with you as you continue your journey.

Below are some journal prompts that will help you during this waning moon ritual:

)   What emotions and thought patterns do I want to release?

)   What limiting beliefs do I want to let go of?

)   What new, reframed beliefs am I embracing?

Reflect on how far you have come and journal about your growth and expansion since the new moon that has past.

Energies to Combine with the Moon Phases

There are other energies – lunar eclipses, supermoons and the star signs – that you can use in combination with the energy of the moon in its different phases. Let's look at these now.

Lunar Eclipse

Eclipses can only take place when the sun, Earth and moon are all aligned. There are four to seven eclipses every calendar year. Usually, there are two eclipse seasons, one after the start of the year and one towards the completion of the year. On a lunar eclipse, the shadow of the Earth falls across the face of the moon bringing unconscious feelings to the surface, such as feeling unworthy, or bringing up old patterns and behaviours. Eclipses are deeply transformative times that can bring abrupt and sudden change, which some may fear, but I see these events as a helping hand of the universe. They will feel more intense than a regular new or full moon.

When I experience a lunar eclipse, it is like the final purge or cleansing of an emotional cycle. I go inwards to be still in the present moment and journal to let go of emotions and attachments that are no longer serving me. If I feel there is something that needs to be gone from my life, if something needs to come to an end, then an eclipse can help me to set the intention of completion.

Eclipses frequently usher in insights and revelations. They serve as the universe's gentle push to realign you with your life's path and guide you towards your intended direction. Eclipses clear away what no longer serves your journey, making room for fresh and exhilarating opportunities to manifest. During an eclipse it is best to make time to sit with your soul, meditate, rest and journal. Listen to your thoughts and get those thoughts out onto paper.

Supermoons

When a full moon or a new moon is closest to Earth in its elliptic orbit, it is called a supermoon. Because the moon appears to be larger and brighter than normal, energetically it is extremely powerful, intense and strongly felt, much like eclipses are. Supermoons will amplify your mood shifts, your personal revelations and your emotional releases.

I use the supermoon for additional clarity. If the new moon is a supermoon, I focus fully on my self-care. If the supermoon is occurring during a full moon, I will focus on releasing my energy. When you are working with the moon in its different phases (new, waxing, full or waning moon), you can weave its energy into your rituals and spell work in the following ways.

New Moon

The new moon is a time of new beginnings, fresh starts and setting intentions. Use this phase to initiate projects, set goals or plant seeds of intention for the upcoming lunar cycle. Perform rituals focused on manifestation, goal-setting and attracting what you desire into your life. Light candles representing your intentions and meditate on your goals, visualizing them coming to fruition.

Waxing Moon

As the moon waxes, its energy is amplifying, making it an ideal time for growth, expansion and manifestation. Continue to work on your intentions set during the new moon, nurturing them as they grow and develop. Perform rituals aimed at increasing abundance, attracting opportunities and enhancing personal development. Charge crystals or other magical tools under the waxing moon to amplify their energy.

Full Moon

The full moon is a time of heightened energy, clarity and illumination. Utilize this phase for releasing, cleansing and celebrating achievements. Perform rituals focused on releasing what no longer serves you, letting go of negativity and embracing gratitude. Charge and cleanse your crystals or magical tools under the full moon's light to enhance their potency. Work with divination tools such as tarot cards or scrying mirrors to gain insights and guidance (*see page 48*).

Waning Moon

As the moon wanes, its energy is decreasing, making it an ideal time for banishing, releasing and clearing away obstacles. Use this phase to let go of negative habits, beliefs or situations that are holding you back. Perform rituals aimed at breaking bad habits, releasing negativity and cutting cords with the past. Cleanse and purify your space using smoke, sound or ritual baths to remove stagnant energy. Practise meditation and introspection to gain clarity and insight into areas of your life that may need releasing or healing.

The Star Signs

You have probably heard phrases like 'the full moon is in Leo', but wondered what that means and how it may affect you. The moon resides in each sign of the zodiac and, as it passes through each sign, it affects us in different ways. By incorporating the wisdom of your specific zodiac sign into your moon phase rituals, you can discern how the moon is guiding you to act and seek guidance aligned with your star sign's energy.

Each star sign comes with its own quality and energy, and each new or full moon will be in a star sign. To find out which zodiac sign the full moon falls under on a specific date, you can simply search 'full moon on [date] zodiac sign' online. The table opposite and overpage, shows the quality of each star sign and the element and energy attached to it.

From new moons that symbolize new beginnings to full moons that amplify our intentions, the magic of the moon phases will have a profound influence on your spellcasting. As you immerse yourself in the enchanting dance of the moon phases, you'll harness its energy to align you back home to yourself.

In the next chapter, you'll discover another layer of magical connection awaiting you – in the realm of plants and herbs. Let the whispers of nature's wisdom continue to guide you on your mystical journey.

Star Sign	Qualities	Element	Energy
Aries	Begin to see the light on the horizon and act on what you want to see change in your life.	Fire	Passion, creativity, motivation
Taurus	Define what feels nourishing and grounding to you. Move into alignment with your worth and follow your inner guide from your soul.	Earth	Grounding, nature, productive
Gemini	Focus your intentions on good communication, change of residence, writing, public relations and travel. This is a good time to benefit from fresh information and new ideas through truly listening to what others have to say.	Air	Communication, inspiration, mental health
Cancer	Slow down, nurture and reawaken your inner world with the luminosity of self-love. It is all about your dreams, intuition, emotions and connection with all.	Water	Intuition, emotion, empathy, wellbeing, spiritual
Leo	Brings forward opportunity, growth and expansion, urging you to embrace your intuition and translate it into decisive action, fostering personal and professional advancement.	Fire	Passion, creativity, motivation

Star Sign	Qualities	Element	Energy
Virgo	An opportunity to clarify and organize your intentions into a plan of success, emphasizing the importance of setting firm boundaries to protect your time, energy and wellbeing, ensuring that your pursuits align with your values and priorities.	Earth	Grounding, nature, productive
Libra	The art of balance and harmony by bringing all points into your perspective. This is a time for self-care and asking yourself what you need to come back into alignment.	Air	Communication, inspiration, mental health
Scorpio	Brings many emotions to the surface, such as old lessons, patterns, thoughts and behaviours that necessitate release and transformation, prompting you to confront and shed what no longer serves your growth and evolution.	Water	Intuition, emotion, empathy, wellbeing, spiritual
Sagittarius	Brings forward a gateway to activate the potential of your power in new and profound ways. All things are possible. Allow expansion.	Fire	Passion, creativity, motivation, desires, energy
Capricorn	This is all about self-responsibility. Now is the time to know your worth, hold your boundaries and commit to your goals.	Earth	Grounding, nature, productive, physical body, sensual

Star Sign	Qualities	Element	Energy
Aquarius	Illuminates higher intellect and visionary insights, presenting opportunities to elevate yourself and contribute to our collective advancement. Tune into the universe's guidance to embrace transformative possibilities and chart a new course aligned with greater purpose and vision.	Air	Communication, inspiration, mental health, thoughts, visioning
Pisces	Illuminates within us the reconciliation to heal that which is out of balance and understanding of our self-worth.	Water	Intuition, emotion, empathy, wellbeing, spiritual

CHAPTER 6

The Magic of Plants

The connection between plants and witches is a profound one, as these magical beings harness the energy and wisdom that emanates from the natural world. Within this chapter, I will guide you through some of the enchanting properties that plants hold for witches, first exploring the top 10 herbs every witch should have in their arsenal, before delving into the magic of trees – ancient sentinels that whisper secrets and offer guidance to those who listen closely.

By tapping into this dimension of energy, you will not only unlock magical and healing qualities, but also gain wisdom and guidance from nature itself. It is through this harmonious union of inner and outer power that true magic is manifested.

Plants

Plants have long been associated with magic and mysticism, and, for centuries, witches have worked with these natural beings to enhance their craft. Witches are often seen as guardians of the

Earth and, by working closely with plants, you can strengthen your bond and foster a deep connection with the natural world.

Working with plants also allows you to tap into the ancient wisdom that resides within these living organisms. Plants have been on this Earth far longer than humans, and they hold within them the knowledge of generations past. By working closely with plants, you can incorporate this knowledge into your magical practices.

Working with plants as a witch is not only a way to connect with nature and access ancient wisdom, but it's also a means of returning home to one's true self. Plants possess a unique energy that resonates with our souls, guiding us back to our primal instincts and intuitive abilities. As you engage in activities such as gardening or herbalism, you will become attuned to the rhythms of nature and learn to listen to its whispers.

Working with plants also allows you to tap into your innate creativity. By spending time tending to plants and nurturing their growth, you are reminded of your own ability to create and manifest change in the world around you.

How to Harness the Power of Plants

The art of herbalism lies at the heart of a witch's practice. From healing ailments to warding off negative energies or attracting love and abundance, plants offer an endless array of possibilities for spellcasting.

Nature has bestowed upon us an abundance of healing powers, waiting to be harnessed through the art of plant-based medicine. By immersing yourself in the study of plants and their properties, you can unlock your potential to combine various herbs to treat a wide range of both physical and spiritual ailments. From soothing teas to potent tinctures, your knowledge will empower you to create concoctions that alleviate physical discomfort and promote overall wellbeing.

As a witch, you can also use herbs in spells to manifest your desires and intentions. Each plant possesses its own unique qualities that can enhance your craft and has distinct energies and associations. During rituals, you can select specific plants based on their symbolic meanings or desired outcomes. Among the myriad of herbs employed in witchcraft, there are 10 that stand out as particularly significant due to their magic and energy:

1. Lavender: plant it for luck, combine it with rosemary to attract love, burn it to bring peacefulness to your home or place it under your pillow to aid in prophetic dreaming.

2. Rosemary: can be successfully substituted for any herb. You can burn rosemary to aid in driving out unwanted energies. It can also be used for purification, healing and love.

3. Cinnamon: used to enhance spirituality, success, luck and prosperity, it can also be used in healing and protection rituals and spells.

4. Mugwort: aids in strengthening psychic powers, dreaming and aural projection. It can also be used for protection and healing. Use it during any other form of divination to increase your psychic awareness.

5. Dandelion: the leaf can be used during divination practices, purification and removing negativity from your home. The root is also used in divination and connecting to your ancestors.

6. Mint: promotes energy, clears the mind, increases communication and stimulates the senses. Mint also attracts money and business, draws in good spirits and protects your home.

7. Lemon balm: used in supporting emotional wellness and the formation of friendships and romantic relationships. It is also a good choice for boosting creativity and for anyone who is working in or studying artistic and creative pursuits.

8. Oregano: used in magic for happiness, tranquillity, clearing negative energy and drain.

9. Bay leaves: used in purifying and cleansing rituals to protect homes/spaces. They are also used in wishes and spells to attract wealth.

10. Cloves: used for protection and can also be used in prosperity spells and friendship charms.

Each herb holds its own unique magic, capable of supporting our physical, emotional and spiritual wellbeing. The process of spellcasting involves carefully blending different plant materials together to create potions or infusions imbued with magical properties. These concoctions are then used in various ways – from anointing candles or talismans to sprinkling around sacred spaces – all designed to amplify the intentions behind the spells.

In modern times, as society becomes increasingly disconnected from nature, exploring the ways in which witches utilize plants serves as a reminder of our interconnectedness with the natural world. It encourages us to appreciate and respect the healing properties present in our surroundings while acknowledging ancient wisdom passed down through the generations.

Embrace the interconnectedness of all things – from plants to trees – as they hold profound lessons waiting to be discovered by those who seek them out.

The Wisdom of the Trees

The other important plants in this earthly dimension are the trees that surround us. Trees hold immense spiritual significance for us witches. They are living beings that possess wisdom and ancient knowledge. I believe that each tree has its own unique energy or spirit that can be tapped into for guidance and support. By communing with trees through meditation or rituals, you can establish a connection with these spirits and gain insight into your own life.

You can also use different parts of trees in your magical workings for their healing properties. The bark, leaves, flowers, fruits, and even the wood itself, can be used for various purposes. For example, willow bark has been used for centuries as a natural remedy for pain relief. Its active ingredient, salicin, acts similarly to aspirin by reducing inflammation and alleviating discomfort. This makes it an attractive alternative for individuals suffering from chronic headaches or back pain who prefer a more holistic approach to managing their symptoms. However, it's important to exercise caution and consult with a healthcare professional before self-prescribing herbal remedies, as they may interact with medications or have unintended side effects, especially for those with pre-existing medical conditions.

In addition to their healing properties, you can also employ trees in divinatory practices such as 'tree scrying' where you can gaze at the patterns formed by leaves or branches against the sky or other reflective surfaces like water. This form of divination allows you to receive messages from the spiritual realm through interpreting symbols or images revealed within the natural patterns.

You may even have heard of people talking to trees. I do this often and find it very relaxing and healing.

HOW TO COMMUNICATE WITH A TREE

1. Find an open space with trees that you love, such as your favourite park, forest or even a spot in your own garden, if you have one.

2. Look around the area and use your intuition to allow yourself to be drawn to a tree.

3. When you first sit down with the tree, take a moment to observe your surroundings. Notice the sounds of birds chirping, the gentle rustling of leaves in the wind or perhaps even the distant sound of flowing water. Pay attention to any sensations you feel in your body. Do you feel grounded or calm? Take a mental note of these details as they can provide valuable insights into your experience.

4. As you begin your attempt at communication, be patient and open-minded. Remember that trees communicate through energy and vibrations rather than words. Allow yourself to be receptive to their messages using your intuition. You may receive images, words or simply a strong intuitive knowing. We'll explore how you can unlock your psychic abilities, such

as clairvoyance, clairaudience and clairsentience in more detail in Chapter 10.

5. Throughout this process, continue paying attention and noticing any changes in your surroundings or within yourself. Is there a shift in energy? Do you feel more connected or attuned? These subtle shifts can indicate that the tree is responding to your presence and attempting to communicate with you.

+ ˙₊⁺✳˙₊⁺ ⋮✳⋮₊⁺˙✳₊⁺˙ +

By asking for permission and being present in your interactions with trees, you can establish a profound connection with nature. The simple act of sitting with a tree and seeking its guidance will allow you to tap into its wisdom and receive valuable insights. Next time you find yourself near a majestic tree, remember to ask if it's okay for you to sit with it and touch it – who knows what incredible messages await you!

Some trees are associated with specific magical properties and are used in spellcasting (*see below*). Furthermore, you can honour these trees through your seasonal celebrations. During the Wheel of the Year (*see Chapter 4*), you can pay homage to the changing seasons by decorating altars with branches or leaves from relevant trees and performing rituals to honour your connection with nature.

The Magical Properties of Trees

I've listed the most common trees and their magical properties below, but these can vary depending on cultural and personal associations, so feel free to explore and connect with the energies of different trees in your magical practice.

- **Apple** – love, fertility, healing, immortality and wisdom

- **Ash** – connection to the world tree, spiritual insight, protection and healing

- **Birch** – purification, new beginnings, growth, fertility and protection

- **Cedar** – purification, protection, grounding and spiritual strength

- **Elder** – healing, protection, prosperity, spirituality and transformation

- **Hawthorn** – protection, love, purification, fertility and healing

- **Hazel** – wisdom, knowledge, divination, protection and creativity

- **Oak** – strength, endurance, protection, wisdom, prosperity, fertility and longevity

- **Pine** – purification, cleansing, prosperity, abundance and rejuvenation

- **Rowan** – protection, divination, psychic abilities and warding off evil

- **Willow** – intuition, psychic abilities, healing, protection, love and fertility

- **Yew** – transformation, death and rebirth, protection and divination

One of my favourite trees is the oak tree. It symbolizes strength, prosperity, protection and overall blessings. The oak tree's essence helps boost energy levels and the ability to manifest goals, as you'll see in the spell below.

ACORN SPELL FOR MANIFESTATION

Acorns are a symbol of good luck, security, vitality, fertility, courage, abundance, prosperity and protection. This spell is ideal if you want to manifest:

> a new job

> a pay rise

> good health

> fertility help

> protection

The perfect time for this spell is: during a new moon or five days after a new moon.

TOOLS

For this spell you will need the following items:

> a mature acorn that has fallen from an oak tree that resonates with you

> your journal and a pen

INSTRUCTIONS

1. First, cleanse the acorn by placing it under running water or burying it in salt overnight.

2. Find a quiet space where you can connect with nature's energy.

3. Hold the cleansed acorn in your hands and clearly visualize your desired outcome.

4. Focus on the emotions associated with achieving this goal and infuse them into the acorn through your touch.

5. Speak aloud your intention while holding the acorn tightly.

6. Once you feel a strong connection between yourself and the acorn, bury it in fertile soil or place it near a tree that represents growth to you. This could be in your garden, if you have one, or in a place you feel you have a connection to.

7. As you do so, express gratitude for the universe's support in manifesting your desires.

8. Document your experiences and insights in your journal, weaving together the wisdom of nature with your own magical journey.

+ . .+ ✦ . + . ✸ . + . .✦ .+. . +

As you continue your journey as a witch, remember to cultivate a deep reverence for nature's gifts. Try planting a magical and spiritual garden to provide a sacred space for your practice and, where you can, draw upon the energies of the plants and herbs you've nurtured. As you do so, they will become your allies, offering their healing properties and guidance.

Now that you have fostered a deep connection with plants, it's time to unlock the magic of animals.

CHAPTER 7

The Magic of Animals

As well as the seasons, the moon phases and the plants, another favourite energy I love to work with is the wisdom of the animal kingdom on Earth. Animals have always held a special place in my heart and I believe that they possess a unique ability to guide us on our spiritual journey.

In this chapter, I will show you how to connect to your animal guide and the signs to look for to tell whether you have a familiar. Animals are powerful messengers from the universe, and they often appear in our lives when we need their guidance or support. By paying attention to their presence and behaviour, we can decipher their messages and gain valuable insights into our own lives.

Animal Guides

Animal guides are spiritual beings that help us navigate through life, providing us with guidance and support. They can appear in many forms, such as dreams, visions or even physical encounters.

Each animal has its own unique symbolism and meaning, which can help us connect with the natural world as well as with our inner selves by providing insight into our personality traits or strengths and weaknesses. For example, if you dream about a lion, it may be a sign that you need to tap into your inner strength and courage to overcome challenges in your life. If you dream about a snake shedding its skin, it may be a sign that you need to let go of old habits or beliefs in order to grow spiritually stronger over time.

I also believe that animals can come forward from our soul family. They could be a reincarnation of a soul we once knew in another lifetime. During my past-life healing sessions that I undertake with my clients, I often hear how they are recalling a lifetime where they were a dog or a bird, or even a mythical creature such as a dragon.

Animals guide us, teach us and communicate with us if we're open enough to listen. In addition to their spiritual symbolism, animal guides can also provide practical guidance for our daily lives. For example, if you are struggling with decision-making or feeling indecisive about something important in your life, consider seeking guidance from an animal guide like the owl who represents wisdom and intuition. To do this, find a quiet outdoor space and clearly set your intentions. Visualize connecting with the owl's spirit in meditation, and reflect on the symbolism associated with owls for insight. Express gratitude for any wisdom received.

Let's now explore the most common animal guides and what they represent.

The butterfly is a symbol of transformation and metamorphosis. Butterflies start as caterpillars, crawling on the ground, but eventually transform into beautiful creatures that can fly. They represent the idea of personal growth and change, reminding us to embrace new beginnings and let go of old patterns that no longer serve us.

The magpie is one of the most superstitious birds and the source of much myth and legend. When it appears, it is calling you to check your priorities. The magpie encourages you not to hide from the world. It wants you to shine your light to everyone you meet, no matter what fears you hold or what others might think.

The owl is an animal guide that represents wisdom and intuition. Owls have keen senses that allow them to see through darkness to find prey or avoid danger; this makes them symbols of insight into hidden truths or the mysteries of life itself. When you repeatedly encounter images of or references to owls, it may be a sign that the owl is trying to communicate with you. Pay attention to these sightings, observe their behaviour and any signs or omens they offer, and reflect on their significance in your life.

The snake is another powerful animal guide that represents transformation and rebirth; snakes regularly shed their skin, which symbolizes shedding old habits or beliefs in order to grow spiritually stronger over time.

The wolf is known for its strength, loyalty and intelligence. Wolves are social animals that live in packs and work together to hunt and protect their territory. In Native American culture, the wolf is seen as a teacher and guide that helps people find their path in life. The wolf represents courage, wisdom and perseverance.

*Animal guides are here to help
guide us in our journeys.*

We are human and it is easy to forget that there is always a universal power that is here to protect us and guide us. Everything we experience in life is a lesson. Guides are here to demonstrate how to get back on track, to show us that we are loved and to remind us to play, create, nurture and connect. As you step into your day, remain aware of your surroundings and notice if any animals keep crossing your path.

Unexpected encounters or sightings of certain animals – known as 'animal omens' – can hold symbolic meaning for us. Animal omens have long been regarded as powerful symbols and messengers in various cultures and spiritual traditions. In Celtic folklore, the appearance of a black cat may be seen as a sign of protection or good luck, while the presence of a raven could signify magic, wisdom or impending transformation. Whether viewed as omens or guides, animals continue to hold a profound and mystical significance in our lives, offering insights and connections to the natural world and the divine. Consider keeping a journal to record your observations and any insights or messages you receive from these animal guides.

Your animal guide could appear in your dreams or people may show you or gift you a certain animal. Another way to access your animal guide is to meditate and ask to see them.

MEET YOUR ANIMAL GUIDE MEDITATION

To embark on this journey, find a quiet and comfortable space where you won't be disturbed. Sit in a relaxed position, either cross-legged on the floor or in a chair with your feet planted firmly on the ground. Close your eyes and take a few deep breaths, allowing yourself to settle into this present moment.

❭ Begin by visualizing yourself standing at the edge of a lush forest. The air is crisp, carrying with it the scent of pine trees and earth. As you step forward into the forest, feel your body becoming lighter and more attuned to nature's rhythms.

❭ As you walk deeper into the woods, notice how sunlight filters through the canopy above, casting dappled shadows on the forest floor. Take in all the sights, sounds and smells around you – every rustle of leaves underfoot or distant birdsong.

❭ Soon enough, you come across a clearing bathed in golden light. In its centre stands an ancient oak tree – tall and majestic – its branches reaching towards the heavens like outstretched arms. Approach this tree with reverence and gratitude for its wisdom.

❭ Place your hands gently on its rough bark as if embracing an old friend. Feel its energy coursing through your fingertips as it connects you to Mother Earth herself. Take another deep breath, inhaling through your nose and exhaling slowly through your mouth.

❭ Now imagine roots growing from your feet deep into the ground below – grounding you firmly in this space between worlds. As these roots anchor you down, feel your body becoming more rooted and centred, ready to receive the guidance of your animal guide.

❯ With this intention in mind, ask silently or aloud for your animal guide to appear. Be patient and open, allowing the universe to bring forth the perfect messenger for you. It may come in the form of a vision, a sensation or even a sound.

❯ As you wait with anticipation, notice any subtle shifts in the energy around you. Pay attention to any thoughts or images that arise – they may hold clues about your animal guide's presence. Trust your intuition and let go of any expectations or preconceived notions.

❯ When you feel ready, slowly open your eyes and take a moment to reflect on your experience. What did you see? How did it make you feel? Take note of any symbols or messages that came through during this meditation – they may hold valuable insights into your life's path. As always, I recommend writing your experiences in your journal.

+ .+ ✳ . + . ✳ . + . ✳ . +

Meeting your animal guide through meditation can provide profound insights and guidance. By connecting with nature on a deeper level like this, you tap into your innate wisdom and intuition. When you find yourself seeking guidance or simply wanting to deepen your spiritual connection, embark on this basic meditation journey and let the animal kingdom lead the way.

A Witch's Familiar

The concept of a witch's familiar has been deeply ingrained in folklore and literature for centuries, captivating the imaginations of readers and enchanting them with tales of extraordinary connections between humans and animals. In particular, cats are traditionally associated with witches and, throughout history, have been linked to magic, mysticism and witchcraft in folklore, literature and art. Cats were believed to possess supernatural powers and were often depicted as familiars or companions to witches. Additionally, during the witch hunts of the Middle Ages, cats were sometimes persecuted alongside suspected witches, further cementing their association with witchcraft. Cats continue to hold a special place in the realm of witchcraft and spirituality for many people today.

In the *Harry Potter* series, J. K. Rowling writes about witches and wizards having animal companions. These creatures play an essential role in assisting their human counterparts in various magical tasks. Rowling cleverly incorporates different types of familiars into her narrative to reflect each character's personality traits. For instance, Harry Potter's owl Hedwig represents loyalty and protection, while Hermione Granger's cat Crookshanks embodies intelligence and resourcefulness. These familiars not only enhance the characters' magical abilities, but also deepen their emotional connections with both their animal companions and readers.

In our modern world, our familiars are loyal guardians and protectors that are usually small household pets. I feel that every witch will most probably have their own familiar, as do I, in the form of a chihuahua called Walter. I believe that familiars are connected to our past lives, they are our truest friend and they understand and know us better than we may even know ourselves. I share a deep spiritual connection with my familiar; we have an innate understanding of one another. It seems like my familiar can read my thoughts and understand my words. His presence comforts me and keeps me grounded.

Here are a few signs to tell if you have your familiar:

- They usually appear in our lives when we need them most. There will be something special that sets them apart from other pets.

- Your familiar is connected to the spirit world dimension. They can sense otherworldly presences and can often detect whether these entities are harmful or benevolent, acting as protectors and guides in navigating these realms. You may recognize your familiar's connection to the spirit world through subtle cues, such as heightened alertness or behaviour changes in the presence of unseen energies, manifestations of protective instincts or reactions, or unexplained occurrences coinciding with your familiar's behaviour, indicating their sensitivity and awareness of spiritual presences.

- Your familiar may exhibit a deep understanding of your emotions and offer comfort during difficult times. They seem to have an innate ability to sense when you need their presence the most, providing solace and support.

- They possess a unique energy that sets them apart from other pets. Whether it's their mesmerizing gaze, mysterious aura or uncanny intuition, there is something undeniably special about them that draws you closer.

- During your spellcasting or rituals, your familiar displays an unwavering desire to be by your side. They may curl up next to you or perch on your shoulder, offering their silent companionship as you delve into the mystical realm.

Having a familiar is a profound connection that goes beyond mere pet ownership. It is a spiritual bond that enriches our lives and provides invaluable assistance on our magical journey. You can utilize your familiar's intuitive guidance, unconditional love and presence as a grounding force to reconnect with your inner self, fostering self-awareness, inner peace and alignment with your path home to self.

Animals serve as messengers in our journey. Their instincts guide us towards self-discovery and offer lessons on adaptability, resilience and interconnectedness. Connecting with our animal spirit guides allows us to tap into ancient wisdom that has been passed down through generations. By embracing these teachings, we can deepen our understanding of ourselves and our place within the natural world. Honouring this sacred relationship allows you to truly return home to your authentic self while recognizing the interconnectedness of all living beings on this Earth.

Immersing yourself in this dimension of the natural world gives you a roadmap for navigating life's ebbs and flows, constantly returning you back to yourself. Just as the changing seasons and moon phases signal when to pause or embrace rebirth, so too does your connection with nature guide you on your spiritual journey. In embracing this understanding, you've unlocked a profound sense of unity with all existence.

Now, armed with this profound connection to the natural world, you are poised to delve even deeper within yourself, unlocking hidden truths and embarking on a transformative inner journey of self-discovery and spiritual growth.

PART III

Learning to Listen to Your Body and Soul

It is so easy to get caught up in the chaos of modern-day life and lose sight of our own wellbeing. We often neglect the importance of taking care of our body and mind, leading to imbalances that can have detrimental effects on our overall health.

To return home to yourself as a witch you must truly look at yourself. 'Doing the work' is the process of getting to know yourself. It's a form of introspective self-care where you can help yourself let go of harmful attachments, habits, people and thoughts. It means taking an honest inventory of who you are and who you want to be.

The journey to being a witch also requires you to confront your fears head-on and delve into the shadows that lurk within your subconscious mind. It is in the dance of the darkness and light that witches learn to embrace both sides of themselves: their strengths as well as their vulnerabilities.

In this part of the book, you will learn all about rebalancing your body, uncovering ways to heal your energy centres and cleanse your aura. Through self-reflection, you will also gain a newfound perspective on your shadows, transforming them into catalysts for growth rather than heavy energy that binds you down. Finally, you'll learn how to raise your vibrational frequency, deepen your intuition and develop your psychic gifts so you can step into your authentic self.

Mistakes are bound to happen along the way; they are part of any learning process. Embrace them as opportunities for growth rather than dwelling on perceived failures. Remember that this journey is about self-discovery and finding your authentic self, returning you home to the witch you are.

The transformation that occurs when embracing your true self is profound. Your body begins to align with your authentic desires, radiating vitality and strength. Your mind becomes clearer, free from the limitations imposed by societal norms and expectations. And your spirit awakens, connecting with ancient wisdom that has always resided within you.

CHAPTER 8

Rebalancing the Body

O ur bodies are not just vessels for our thoughts and emotions; they are intricate systems that hold valuable information. When we ignore the signals they send us, we miss out on important insights that can guide us through life's complexities. Our bodies act as compasses, pointing us in the right direction if we learn to listen.

In this chapter, you'll learn the tools to pay attention to how your body feels and acts, exploring your energy centres and how they can be healed and unlocked, as well as how to cleanse your aura to enhance your connection to higher realms of consciousness. As you embark on this journey, you'll discover that this process is deeply intertwined with your physical wellbeing. By nurturing and balancing your energy centres, you not only promote harmony within your body, mind and spirit, but also facilitate a deeper connection with your inner self. This holistic approach to healing allows you to come home to yourself on a profound level, fostering inner peace, self-awareness and alignment with your authentic essence.

Healing Your Energy Centres

Energy centres, also known as chakras, are a fundamental part of various ancient healing practices. They are believed to be located along the body's central axis and are associated with different aspects of our physical, emotional and spiritual wellbeing. When these energy centres are balanced and flowing freely, we experience harmony and vitality in our lives. However, when they become blocked or imbalanced, it can lead to various physical and emotional ailments.

In traditional Chinese medicine, the concept of energy centres is closely related to the flow of Qi, or life force, through meridians in the body. By balancing and harmonizing these energy centres, practitioners aim to restore health and promote overall wellbeing.

Similarly, in Ayurvedic medicine from India, chakras are seen as vital energy wheels that govern our physical and mental functions. Through techniques such as meditation, yoga and specific dietary practices, Ayurvedic healers seek to activate and balance the chakras to achieve optimal health.

While modern science may not fully understand or acknowledge the existence of chakras yet, many people continue to find solace and healing through these ancient practices. The exploration of energy centres offers a holistic approach towards wellness that encompasses mind, body and spirit – a timeless wisdom worth exploring in our modern world.

Root Chakra

This is the first energy centre and is located at the base of the spine. The root chakra is associated with our sense of stability, security and connection to the Earth. Signs of imbalance in the root chakra include:

- feelings of insecurity, fear, anxiety or instability

- financial difficulties

- lack of grounding

- lower back pain or issues with the legs and feet

- digestive problems

To heal this centre, grounding exercises, such as walking barefoot on grass or sand, can be highly effective and allow us to connect directly with the Earth's energy. Additionally, practising yoga poses such as 'mountain pose' or 'tree pose' helps to strengthen our connection to the ground.

Sacral Chakra

Moving up the spine, the sacral chakra is situated just below the navel. This chakra governs our creativity and sexuality. Signs of imbalance in the sacral chakra include:

- emotional instability or mood swings

- creative blockages

- issues with intimacy or relationships

- reproductive issues

- lower abdominal discomfort or pain

One powerful technique for healing this centre is through creative expression, such as painting or writing poetry. Engaging in activities that bring joy and pleasure also helps balance this chakra.

Solar Plexus Chakra

Next is the solar plexus chakra located in the upper abdomen area. This chakra represents personal power and self-confidence. Signs of imbalance in the solar plexus chakra include:

● lack of self-confidence or self-esteem

● difficulty making decisions

● feeling powerless or victimized

● digestive issues or stomach ulcers

● tension in the abdomen or upper back

Breathing exercises like deep belly breathing can help activate this centre by increasing oxygen flow to it. Visualization techniques where one envisions a bright yellow light radiating from the solar plexus can also aid in healing.

Heart Chakra

This resides in the centre of our chest and represents love and compassion towards ourselves and others. Signs of imbalance in the heart chakra include:

● difficulty in giving or receiving love

- feelings of loneliness or isolation

- holding grudges or resentment

- heart palpitations or chest tightness

- respiratory issues or asthma

To heal emotional wounds or enhance your ability to give and receive love, try the spell below. As you continue practising this spell regularly over time, you may find that it becomes easier for you to connect with others on a deeper level. You may notice an increased capacity for empathy and compassion, as well as a greater ability to forgive and let go of past hurts.

OPEN THE *HEART* CENTRE SPELL

The intention of this spell is to open the heart space to receive.

The perfect time for this spell is: during a new moon.

TOOLS

For this spell you will need the following items:

- matches

- a cleansing tool such as incense, a smoke wand or resin

- a small bowl of white salt, enough so that a candle can stand within the dish

- a small pink or white candle

> ❯ a small knife or pin to scratch the candle

> ❯ rose quartz crystal

> ❯ dried lavender

> ❯ rose petals or rose buds

> ❯ a pen and a piece of A4 paper

> ❯ a cauldron or fireproof container

> ❯ a small glass jar with a lid

ℐNSTRUCTIONS

1. Find a quiet and peaceful space where you can be alone. It is important to create an environment that feels safe and sacred, as this will help facilitate the opening of the heart chakra.

2. Gather your tools and smoke-cleanse yourself, your tools and the space that you are in.

3. Begin by taking several deep breaths, allowing yourself to relax and let go of any tension or stress.

4. Place the dish of salt in front of you. Using the knife or pin, scratch words related to love, self-love and healing into your candle. Choose empowering words such as 'I love me', 'I am worthy', 'I am beautiful' or 'I can achieve all of my desires'. Then place the candle into the middle of the salt.

5. Place the rose quartz near the dish and sprinkle the lavender onto the salt in a clockwise direction. Do the same with the rose petals/buds.

6. Close your eyes and visualize a bright green light at the centre of your chest. This light represents your heart chakra.

7. As you continue to breathe deeply, imagine this green light expanding with each inhale, filling your entire chest cavity. Feel it radiating warmth and

love throughout your body. Allow yourself to fully immerse in these feelings of love and compassion.

8. Next, recite the following incantation, focusing on each word as you say it. Feel the energy of these words resonating within you, strengthening your intention to open your heart centre.

   By the power within me, I open my heart centre wide.
   May love flow freely from me, And may I receive it in return.

   By the power within me, I open my heart centre wide.
   May love flow freely from me, And may I receive it in return.

   By the power within me, I open my heart centre wide.
   May love flow freely from me, And may I receive it in return.

   So it is.

9. After reciting the incantation, take a moment to sit in silence and observe any sensations or emotions that arise within you. Notice if there are any areas of resistance or blockages in your heart centre. If so, gently breathe into these areas. Open your eyes and write down any words that you wish to let go of on the piece of paper. Fold the paper away from yourself.

10. When you are ready, place the paper into the candle flame and straight into the cauldron or fireproof container to burn away.

11. Looking at the flames, imagine them melting away with each exhale.

12. The cooled ashes can be used in a bath, added to plants in your home or kept with the salt, the last part of the candle and the other ingredients in a small glass jar to create a spell jar.

It is important to remember that this spell is not a quick fix or a magic cure-all. It is a practice that requires dedication and patience. Opening the heart chakra is a journey, and it may take time for you to fully experience its effects.

In addition to practising this spell, it can also be helpful to engage in other activities that promote love and connection. This could include acts of kindness towards others, spending time in nature or engaging in creative pursuits that bring you joy. Practising the forgiveness meditation below is also an effective technique for healing this centre as it allows you to release any resentment or grudges you may hold on to.

Simple Forgiveness Meditation

Find a quiet and comfortable space to sit or lie down. Close your eyes and take a few deep breaths to centre yourself.

Bring to mind someone you wish to forgive. This could be yourself or another person who has caused you pain or difficulty.

Visualize this person in your mind's eye and imagine them standing before you. Take a moment to acknowledge any emotions that arise.

Repeat the following affirmations silently or aloud:

I forgive you.
I release any anger or resentment I hold towards you.
I choose to let go of the past and move
forward with love and compassion.

As you continue to breathe deeply, visualize any negative energy or emotions surrounding the situation dissolving away, leaving you feeling lighter and more at peace.

Finally, extend forgiveness to yourself if needed, repeating the affirmations:

I forgive myself.
I release any guilt or shame I hold towards myself.
I choose to embrace self-love and compassion.

Take a few more deep breaths, allowing yourself to fully absorb the feelings of forgiveness and compassion. When you're ready, gently open your eyes and return to the present moment.

+ ˙ ₊ ✦ ˙ ₊ ˙ ✸ ˙ ₊ ˙ ✦ ₊ ˙ ₊

Throat Chakra

The throat chakra is located at the base of our throat. This chakra governs communication and self-expression. Signs of imbalance in the throat chakra include:

- difficulty expressing oneself
- fear of speaking up or being heard
- throat tightness or discomfort
- thyroid issues
- frequent sore throats or coughing

Singing or chanting can help open and balance this centre. Additionally, practising mindful listening and speaking with authenticity can aid in healing this chakra.

How to Listen Mindfully

● Be fully present: focus your attention on the speaker without distractions. Avoid interrupting or formulating your response while they're speaking.

● Listen with empathy: seek to understand the speaker's perspective and emotions. Reflect back what you hear to ensure you've understood correctly.

● Let go of judgements: release preconceived notions or biases and approach the conversation with an open mind and heart.

● Stay non-reactive: practise observing your own reactions and emotions without immediately responding. Allow space for silence and reflection.

How to Speak with Authenticity

● Connect with your truth: keeping your truth bottled up can lead to stress, anxiety and emotional distress. Before speaking, take a moment to tune into your thoughts, feelings and intentions. Speak from a place of honesty and integrity. Speaking your truth is crucial for personal growth and authenticity, and allows you to release pent-up emotions and cultivate emotional wellbeing.

● Express yourself clearly: use clear and concise language to convey your message. Be mindful of your tone and body language, ensuring they align with your words.

◐ Share openly: be willing to share your thoughts, feelings and experiences authentically, even if they feel vulnerable or uncomfortable.

◐ Listen to your intuition: trust your inner wisdom and intuition when communicating. If something doesn't feel right, honour that feeling and adjust your approach accordingly.

◐ Practise active listening: engage in actively listening to others and responding thoughtfully. Validate their experiences and perspectives, even if you disagree.

Third Eye Chakra

This chakra is situated between the eyebrows and represents intuition and inner wisdom. Signs of imbalance in the third eye chakra include:

◐ lack of clarity or intuition

◐ feeling disconnected from one's inner wisdom

◐ headaches or migraines

◐ vision problems or eye strain

◐ difficulty concentrating or making decisions

Meditation is a powerful technique for healing this centre as it allows you to quieten the mind and tap into your intuitive abilities. Visualization exercises where you envision an indigo light expanding from the third eye can also be beneficial.

Crown Chakra

Finally, the crown chakra sits at the top of our head and connects us to higher consciousness and spiritual enlightenment. Signs of imbalance in the crown chakra include:

◑ feeling disconnected from spirituality or higher consciousness

◑ lack of purpose or meaning in life

◑ depression or existential crisis

◑ issues with the central nervous system

◑ migraines or light sensitivity

Practising gratitude is a simple yet profound technique for healing this centre. Taking time each day to reflect on what you are grateful for helps to open this chakra and connect you to something greater than yourself. See page 152 for more on gratitude practices.

Engaging in activities that bring joy and laughter helps maintain energetic balance.

It is important to note that healing your energy centres is an ongoing process that requires patience and self-awareness. It may take time to identify blockages or imbalances within each centre, but, with consistent practice, you can gradually restore harmony within your body.

In addition to the specific techniques outlined above, there are general practices that support overall energetic balance. Regular physical exercise helps keep energy flowing smoothly throughout the body, while eating a healthy diet rich in fruits, vegetables and whole grains provides essential nutrients that support optimal energy flow.

By tapping into your energy centres you can channel positive energies into all aspects of your life. This not only enhances your wellbeing but also empowers you to set intentions in your magical practices as a witch.

Cleansing Your Aura

We all possess a unique energy field that emanates from our physical body, known as the aura. Understanding your aura helps you return home to your body by deepening your awareness of the subtle energy field that surrounds and permeates your physical form. As you learn to recognize and interpret the messages encoded within your aura, you become more attuned to the sensations and energetic fluctuations within your body. This heightened awareness fosters a deeper connection with your physical vessel, allowing you to embody a greater sense of presence and authenticity. By nurturing this connection through practices such as meditation, energy healing and mindful movement, you return back to your body.

The human aura appears as a luminous glow or halo around the body. It is said to consist of different layers or levels that correspond to different aspects of our being. These layers are seen in colours, each carrying its own significance and representing different aspects of our personality, emotions and spiritual wellbeing:

◑ The outermost layer is commonly referred to as the etheric body and is believed to be associated with physical health and vitality. It is often depicted as a pale blue colour.

◑ The next layer is known as the emotional body, which reflects our emotions and feelings; it may appear in various shades depending on our current emotional state.

◑ The mental body, which represents our thoughts and intellectual capacity, is the next layer and is often depicted in yellow hues symbolizing clarity and intellectuality.

◑ Finally, at the core of our being lies what some call the spiritual body, which is associated with our higher consciousness and connection to the divine. This layer is often described as a brilliant white or golden light.

The Significance of Aura Colours

These ethereal hues given off by the body are not mere figments of imagination, but rather a reflection of an individual's spiritual and emotional state. Each colour pulsates with its own unique significance, offering glimpses into the depths of one's being. A vivid red hue, for instance, signifies passion and vitality, exuding an intense energy that ignites the flames within. It represents a fiery nature, burning with desire and ambition. In contrast, a cool blue hue emanates a tranquil aura that soothes the soul like gentle waves caressing a serene shore. It symbolizes clarity of thought and communication, fostering calmness amidst chaos.

Moving beyond these primary colours lies an array of shades that add layers to our understanding of human nature. A vibrant orange aura suggests enthusiasm and creativity; it is the colour of inspiration that drives artists to create masterpieces brimming with life. Similarly, a luminous yellow aura signifies intelligence and optimism; it is the radiance that enlightens minds and illuminates paths in times of darkness.

However, not all colours bear positive connotations – some hint at inner turmoil and pain. A murky grey hue embodies feelings of confusion and ambiguity, a nebulous fog obscuring clarity from sight. It reflects indecisiveness and uncertainty as one navigates through life's labyrinthine corridors searching for answers.

Shades such as deep purple or rich indigo possess an air of mystique around them and are colours associated with spirituality and intuition. They represent individuals who possess innate wisdom beyond their years; these people are often regarded as seers or mystics who can peer into realms invisible to ordinary eyes.

It is essential to acknowledge that aura colours are not static but ever-changing entities influenced by emotions and experiences. For instance, when engulfed in rage or anger, one's aura might transform into a fiery crimson, radiating a destructive energy that can consume everything in its path. Conversely, moments of deep sorrow may manifest as a dull grey or even black, signifying the weight of grief that engulfs the spirit.

Techniques for Cleansing Your Aura

Negative energies can cling to our aura due to daily stressors or interactions with others. These energies can disrupt the flow of vital life force energy within us, leading to imbalances in physical health or emotional wellbeing. Cleansing your aura helps remove these stagnant energies.

Cleansing your aura not only promotes spiritual wellbeing, but also contributes to overall physical health, as a balanced and purified energetic field supports the body's natural ability to maintain harmony and vitality. Embrace these practices with an open heart and witness the profound impact they have on cleansing and revitalizing your aura:

● Smoke-cleansing: burning sacred herbs like sage or palo santo creates smoke that can purify your aura by dispelling negative energies.

● Salt baths: taking a bath infused with sea salt or Epsom salt helps draw out impurities from your energetic field.

● Visualization: imagine a bright light surrounding you, gradually dissolving any dark or heavy energy present in your aura.

● Sound healing: listening to soothing music or using instruments like singing bowls can help release stagnant energy and restore balance.

● Nature connection: spending time in nature, whether it's walking in a forest or sitting by the ocean, can cleanse and rejuvenate your aura.

● Reiki or energy healing: seek the assistance of a trained practitioner who can channel healing energy to cleanse and balance your aura.

Cleansing your aura is not a one-time event, but an ongoing practice. Regular self-care activities such as meditation, yoga or journaling can help maintain the purity of your energetic field. Surround yourself with positive people and environments that uplift your spirit. Engage in activities that bring you joy and nourish your soul. By consciously cultivating positive energy within yourself, you create a protective shield around your aura.

By cleansing your aura and aligning your energy centres you have unlocked a power that can be harnessed in your daily life. You are now ready for the next chapter, which is all about embracing your true self.

CHAPTER 9

Clarifying the Mind

In this chapter, I am going to guide you through the transformative journey of connecting with your authentic self. Embracing your true essence is an important step towards harnessing your power as a witch. Clarifying the mind is a vital aspect of this journey, as it allows you to quieten the noise of external influences and connect with your inner wisdom and intuition. By clearing away mental clutter and distractions, you create space to explore your deepest desires, beliefs and intentions, paving the way for profound self-discovery and empowerment.

Embrace this journey wholeheartedly because it is only by standing firmly in who you are that you can truly unlock the magic within you. Finding your authentic self is about understanding what makes you unique, and it all starts with self-reflection.

Self-Reflection

Moments of self-reflection allow you to contemplate the experiences that have shaped you – both positive and negative

– and how they have influenced your identity. By questioning societal expectations and cultural norms imposed upon you since birth, you can begin to separate your genuine desires from those dictated by others.

Journaling can be a powerful tool in this journey of self-discovery. By working through the prompts below, you can delve deep into your thoughts and emotions, uncovering the essence of who you truly are. Grab a pen and start journaling.

SELF-REFLECTION JOURNAL PROMPTS

WHAT BRINGS ME JOY?

Take a moment to reflect on the activities or experiences that make your heart sing. Is it spending time in nature? Creating art? Connecting with loved ones? Whatever it may be, write about why these things bring you joy and how they align with your values and passions so that you can prioritize these activities and ensure that you are living authentically.

WHAT ARE MY CORE VALUES?

Our values shape our beliefs, decisions and actions. Take some time to reflect on what truly matters to you. Is it honesty? Compassion? Freedom? Write about why these values resonate with you and how they guide your choices in life. When you live in alignment with your core values, you feel more fulfilled and content.

WHAT ARE MY FEARS?

Fear often holds us back from fully expressing ourselves or pursuing our dreams. By acknowledging and exploring our fears through journaling, we can better understand their origins and begin to overcome them. Write about your deepest fears – whether they are related to failure, rejection or vulnerability – and reflect on how they have influenced your choices thus far. Recognizing these fears allows you to move past them and live a more authentic life. (We'll explore how to release these fears next.)

WHAT ARE MY DREAMS AND ASPIRATIONS?

Our dreams are often a reflection of our true desires and passions. Take some time to write about the things you have always wanted to do or achieve. Whether it is travelling the world, starting your own business or writing a book, allow yourself to dream big. Reflect on why these dreams are important to you and how they align with your values and purpose. By acknowledging your dreams, you can take steps towards making them a reality.

$$+ \cdot \cdot_+ * \cdot \cdot + \cdot \ast \cdot + \cdot \ast_+ \cdot \cdot +$$

This journey of self-discovery is an ongoing process that requires patience and dedication. It invites you to make peace with both the light and darker aspects of yourself while embracing expansion along the way.

To step into your true self, you must also gain clarity on your fears and start dismantling their hold on you. Please take this next part of the journey with ease – go gentle on yourself as it may bring up some old wounds.

Removing Blocks and Fears

Fear can be a powerful force that holds us back from fully embracing our magic, but, through introspection and reflection, we can confront these fears head-on and overcome them. Our fears and resistance often serve as indicators pointing us towards our greatest expansion. It is through acknowledging and moving through these that we discover the most valuable lessons. I have learned that the bigger the resistance you have over something your intuition is guiding you to do, the bigger the shift in your life if you head into that resistance.

Without resistance,
there is no growth.

The world around us shows us this within nature – when the leaves fall, new growth returns. Facing your fears and embracing what your soul truly desires, despite the resistance, will activate a creative power within you.

Again, journaling is an effective tool for exploring your fears and finding ways to overcome them. Below are some journal prompts to help you release the fears that are holding you back.

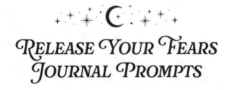

RELEASE YOUR FEARS JOURNAL PROMPTS

WHAT IS MY BIGGEST FEAR?

Take some time to reflect on what scares you the most in life. Is it a fear of failure? Rejection? Success? Write about why this fear holds such power over you and how it has impacted your life so far. By acknowledging your fear, you are taking the first step towards releasing its hold on you.

CWHEN DID CI FACE ONE OF MY FEARS HEAD-ON?

Describe the situation in detail. How did it make you feel? What actions did you take to confront your fear? Reflect on how this experience changed you and what lessons you learned from it. By revisiting moments of courage in your past, you can gain confidence in facing future challenges.

CWHAT WOULD LIFE LOOK LIKE IF FEAR DIDN'T HOLD ME BACK?

Imagine all the things you would do if there were no limitations or doubts. Write about your dreams, goals and aspirations without the interference of fear. Visualize yourself acting towards these dreams and achieving them. By envisioning a fearless future, you can start to manifest it in your present.

+ · ₊ ✳ · ₊ · ✳ · ₊ · ✳ ₊ · ₊

Now you have started to release the fears holding you back, it's time to look at the parts of yourself you may have repressed or denied – known as your shadow self.

Healing Your Shadow Self

You may have heard of the 'shadow self' or 'shadow work'. The shadow is composed of both positive and negative aspects. It includes our fears, insecurities and desires, and even our hidden talents and potential. These aspects are typically hidden from our conscious awareness because they do not align with our self-image or societal expectations – our shadow self represents the parts of ourselves that we have repressed or denied. However, they still influence our thoughts, emotions and behaviours.

Engaging in shadow work can be a transformative process that allows us to gain a deeper understanding of ourselves and ultimately lead more fulfilling lives. By shining a light on these dark corners of our psyche, we can integrate them into our sense of self instead of allowing them to control us unconsciously. We can also tap into hidden strengths and talents, and achieve wholeness.

Below are some steps to get started with your shadow self. Engaging in shadow work can be challenging and emotionally intense. Consider seeking the guidance of a therapist or joining a support group to navigate this process.

Self-reflection: begin by setting aside time for introspection. Find a quiet space where you can reflect on your thoughts and emotions without distractions. Ask yourself what parts of yourself you may have been avoiding or denying.

Journaling: writing down your thoughts and feelings can be an effective way to explore your inner world. Use your journal to record any insights or observations that arise during your self-reflection sessions.

Identifying triggers: pay attention to situations or people who trigger strong emotional reactions within you. These triggers often point towards unresolved issues within your shadow self.

Dream analysis: dreams often provide valuable insights into our unconscious mind. Keep a dream journal and analyse the symbols and themes that appear in your dreams. They may offer clues about unresolved issues within your shadow self.

Creative expression: engage in creative activities such as painting, writing or dancing to tap into your unconscious mind.

Allow yourself to express emotions and thoughts that may have been suppressed.

Shadow integration: once you have identified aspects of your shadow self, work on integrating them into your conscious awareness. This involves acknowledging their presence without acting on them impulsively or repressing them further.

Self-compassion: be gentle with yourself throughout this process. It is natural to encounter resistance or discomfort when exploring the shadow, but remember that it is an essential part of personal growth. Recognize that everyone has both light and dark sides; it is part of being human.

Continued practice: shadow work is an ongoing process that requires consistent effort and self-reflection. Make it a habit to regularly check in with yourself and explore any emerging shadows.

Engaging in this transformative process allows you to embrace all parts of yourself without judgement or shame while creating space for personal growth and transformation.

$\mathcal{S}$ELF-LOVE$\mathcal{S}$PELL

Here is a self-love spell that you can perform in any season. By practising self-love, you can build resilience, improve relationships with others and ultimately lead a fulfilling life. It is an essential journey towards self-acceptance and personal growth.

The perfect time for this spell is: full moon, retrograde, eclipse.

TOOLS

For this spell you will need the following items:

- a pestle and mortar
- two pinches of dried rose petals
- a pinch of dried thyme and rosemary
- five whole cloves
- a pinch of ground cinnamon
- a pinch of frankincense resin
- matches
- a charcoal disc
- a cauldron or fireproof container

INSTRUCTIONS

1. Using the pestle and mortar, blend all the herbs and resin in a clockwise direction, thinking of love surrounding you.

2. Place your left hand on your heart and feel your breath.

3. Call forward your ancestors with the highest good, love and light to be close to you. Feel their love and support around you.

4. Light the charcoal disc and place it into the cauldron or fireproof container and add a pinch of the herbs, saying, 'I am loved, I am enough.'

5. Over the next days and week, look out for special signs from the universe, such as feathers, animals or numbers that appear on your daily path.

As you delve into the depths of your psyche during shadow work, you confront and release limiting beliefs, fears and patterns that have kept you from fully embracing your witchy essence. This process clears the path for reprogramming your mind, where you actively replace old, disempowering thought patterns with new, empowering ones aligned with your inner witch.

Reprogramming the Subconscious Mind

This is a pivotal step on your journey to uncovering your true self as a witch. Your subconscious is the part of your mind that makes decisions without you needing to actively think about them. It is constantly absorbing information from outside sources and using that information to form beliefs that shape how you think and behave.

Your thoughts shape your reality, and negativity from the daily news, toxic people and social media can have a profound effect on your subconscious mind. It is therefore crucial to consciously choose positive thoughts and replace limiting beliefs with empowering ones using the steps below:

Gain clarity: absolute clarity on what it is you want brings power. The more thought you put into the detail, the stronger your vision will become. This gives your brain the tools necessary to turn that vision into reality.

Take action: lack of action gives negative thoughts time to stay stuck in your mind. Learn from your mistakes, embrace failure and use negativity as a direction of expansion.

Let go: you cannot control your life. The only thing you can control is your actions and reactions. Focus on trust in yourself and in the universe. By living consciously – being fully present and aware in every moment, and making deliberate choices that align with your values, intentions and higher purpose – you can let go and enjoy life.

Practise gratitude: when you practise gratitude over criticism, you will rewire your brain to notice more of what you have and less of what you don't.

Create your environment: surround yourself with positive, supportive people. Seek out people, books, videos and music that lift you up and empower you. You will find that, over time, your subconscious mind is more positive and encouraging and that negative thoughts have greatly diminished.

Visualize: pick something you are truly committed to making a reality and spend 10–15 minutes each day visualizing it as if it has already happened. Your subconscious mind will absorb the feelings in your images as if they were real, giving you the inner confidence you need to make them come true.

Work on mindset: cultivate positive beliefs and affirmations that align with your magical intentions and create a mindset that supports you in manifesting your desires.

10 Positive Affirmations

- ◐ 'I am a powerful creator, and my magic flows effortlessly through me.'

- ◐ 'I trust in the divine timing of the universe to manifest my desires.'

- ◐ 'I am deserving of abundance, love and all good things that come my way.'

- ◐ 'My thoughts are aligned with my intentions, and I manifest my dreams with ease.'

- ◐ 'I am surrounded by positive energy, and I attract positivity into my life.'

- ◐ 'I release all fear and doubt, knowing that I am supported by the universe.'

- ◐ 'I am connected to the wisdom of the Earth, and I trust in its guidance.'

- ◐ 'I embrace my inner witch and celebrate my unique magical gifts.'

- ◐ 'I am in harmony with the cycles of nature, and I align with their rhythms.'

- ◐ 'I am grateful for the magic that surrounds me, and I embrace its infinite possibilities.'

By harnessing techniques such as affirmations, visualization and meditation, you embed beliefs that resonate with your true nature, empowering you to step into your magic with confidence and authenticity. Each step in this chapter – self-reflection, removing blocks and fears, shadow work and reprogramming the mind – is a vital component on your journey towards self-discovery and empowerment, guiding you towards alignment with your true self and the realization of your witchy potential.

Throughout this journey, we've explored the depths of the natural and inner worlds, discovering how to harness their guidance as you step into your emerging identity as a witch. In the next chapter, we'll focus on reclaiming your power, infusing it into your heart and soul. You are about to discover how to connect to your most powerful self.

Calling Back Your Power

This chapter serves as a culmination of your journey thus far, focusing on reclaiming and harnessing your innate power as a witch. Calling back your power involves reclaiming the energy and essence that you may have unconsciously scattered or relinquished throughout your life due to societal conditioning, past trauma or self-limiting beliefs. As a witch, reclaiming your power means embodying your magical potential to create positive change in your life and the world around you. This chapter will guide you through practices and insights to help you step into your inherent power with confidence and sovereignty, aligning your energy with your highest intentions and aspirations.

The most important step in calling back your power is identifying and raising the frequency that you vibrate at.

The Self Frequency

We often find ourselves constantly connected to our devices, overwhelmed with information and surrounded by noise. We are always on the go, multitasking and striving for success in every aspect of our lives. We are bombarded with news updates, advertisements and opinions from all directions. This can be mentally exhausting and makes it challenging for us to filter out what is truly important and relevant to our lives.

Surrounded by noise both literally and metaphorically, it has become increasingly difficult for us to disconnect from the outside world and find moments of peace and quiet in our lives. We are constantly checking emails, scrolling through social media feeds and responding to notifications. This never-ending chatter and stimulation can lead to increased stress levels and decreased mental clarity, and prevents us from truly connecting with ourselves on a deeper level. It is crucial for us to recognize the impact that this constant connectivity has on our wellbeing.

I want to now help you take a step back from this constant connectivity and noise. By doing so, you can reconnect with your own frequency – one that promotes wellness and balance, which will help you to set intentions and connect to the dimensions around you and within you, which we'll explore in the next part of the book.

Identifying Your Frequency

There are two frequencies that we vibrate at:

1. Low vibrations, such as fear, shame, guilt or anger.

2. High vibrations, such as love, joy or abundance.

Whichever frequency you are vibrating at, that is what you are attracting into your life. When we operate from a place of low vibrations, we emit a frequency that resonates with these negative emotions. Consequently, we draw experiences and people into our lives that align with these lower vibrations. It becomes a vicious cycle where negativity breeds more negativity.

On the other hand, when we vibrate at higher frequencies, our energy attracts positive experiences and like-minded individuals who resonate with these frequencies. We become magnets for happiness and success. Understanding this principle will allow you to take control of your life by consciously choosing the frequency at which you vibrate.

Take a moment now to reflect on the areas of your life where you feel disempowered or drained. Is it in your relationships? Your career? Your personal goals? Identify the specific situations or individuals that make you feel powerless. This self-reflection will help you gain clarity about what needs to change.

Ways to Raise Your Vibration

Once you have identified the sources of disempowerment in your life, it is important to set boundaries. Boundaries are essential for protecting your energy and wellbeing. There have likely been occasions when you've had plans for yourself, only to be contacted by a friend or family member asking for help or to meet up. In that moment, your true soul's vibration shines through, often feeling like a resolute 'no' to deviating from your plans. However, your mind may interject and you end up agreeing to change your plans because you seek validation or fear upsetting others. Remember that setting boundaries does not make you selfish; it simply means that you value yourself enough to protect your own needs. Clearly define what is acceptable and unacceptable behaviour from others and communicate your boundaries assertively but respectfully.

Another crucial step in raising your vibration is being more aware of yourself and how you are feeling. Negative thoughts and emotions can lower our vibrational energy levels, leading to increased stress and decreased immune function. On the other hand, positive thoughts and emotions raise our vibrational energy levels, promoting overall wellbeing. By identifying the negative patterns that are keeping you stuck in low vibrations, you can begin to shift them towards higher frequencies. Recognize that you have control over how you respond to external circumstances. Choose empowering thoughts and actions that align with who you truly are.

In today's fast-paced and materialistic world, it is easy to get caught up in the never-ending pursuit of more. We are constantly bombarded with messages that tell us we need the latest gadgets, the trendiest clothes and the biggest houses to be happy. This constant focus on what is lacking in our lives can leave us feeling unsatisfied and unfulfilled. However, there is a simple yet powerful practice that can help shift our perspective and further raise our vibration – gratitude. Gratitude is the act of acknowledging and appreciating the good things in our lives, big or small. It is about recognizing the blessings we already have rather than dwelling on what we lack.

When we cultivate an attitude of gratitude, something magical happens. Our focus shifts from scarcity to abundance, from negativity to positivity. We notice all the little things that bring us joy – a beautiful sunset, a warm cup of coffee in the morning or a kind word from a friend. By shifting our attention to these positive experiences, we attract more of them into our lives.

Moreover, practising gratitude fosters a sense of contentment within us. Instead of constantly striving for more, we learn to appreciate and be satisfied with what we already have. This sense of contentment brings peace and tranquillity into our lives.

Gratitude also enhances relationships by fostering deeper connections with others. When we express gratitude towards someone for their kindness or support, it strengthens the bond between us. It creates a positive energy that raises our frequency and attracts more love and kindness into our relationships.

Finally, practising gratitude promotes overall wellbeing and happiness. Numerous studies have shown that grateful people experience lower levels of stress and depression while enjoying higher levels of optimism and life satisfaction.

Another practice I have found useful in reconnecting with what is truly important is, again, meditation and deep breathing exercises. These practices allow us to let go of negative thoughts or worries about the future while reducing stress levels. By consciously creating space for silence in your life – whether through meditation or simply spending time alone – you can regain focus and prioritize what really matters. By regularly engaging in mindfulness activities, we increase our vibrational energy levels while improving mental clarity and emotional stability.

The people we surround ourselves with also play a significant role in influencing our own frequency. Have you ever noticed how spending time with certain individuals leaves you feeling drained or exhausted? This phenomenon happens because we are energetically connected to those around us. If we spend time with negative or toxic individuals, their low vibrational energy can affect our own frequency, leading to a decline in our overall wellness.

In contrast, being in the presence of positive and uplifting people can have a profound impact on our wellbeing. These people radiate high vibrational energy, which can elevate our own frequency and promote feelings of joy, love and peace.

Evaluate the relationships in your life and identify those that drain your energy or make you feel disempowered. Limit your interactions with these individuals or, if necessary, cut ties altogether. Instead, seek out relationships that uplift and inspire you. Surrounding yourself with like-minded individuals who support your growth and encourage you to be the best version of yourself will help you reclaim your power. It's important to keep close those who bring you ease, positivity and support, as they can uplift and inspire you on your journey through life. Choosing your inner circle wisely can make all the difference in your personal growth.

Remember, though, that true power comes from within; it is not dependent on external circumstances or other people's opinions. Embrace the journey of reclaiming your power with patience and compassion for yourself using the protection spell below.

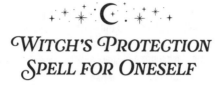

WITCH'S PROTECTION
SPELL FOR ONESELF

This spell not only shields you from negative energy, but also empowers you with inner strength and resilience.

The perfect time for this spell is: full moon or three days after a new moon.

TOOLS

For this spell you will need the following items:

> matches

> a cleansing tool such as incense, a smoke wand or resin

> a white candle

> a small piece of black tourmaline or obsidian crystal (known for their protective properties)

> dried rosemary leaves (for purification)

> lavender essential oil (for calming energy)

> a small fabric pouch or bag to hold these items

INSTRUCTIONS

1. To begin this spell, find a quiet space where you can focus your energy without distractions.

2. Smoke-cleanse yourself, your tools and the space that you are in.

3. Light the candle and place it in front of you.

4. Take a moment to ground yourself by taking deep breaths and visualizing roots growing from your feet into the earth.

5. Next, gather the black tourmaline or obsidian crystal, dried rosemary leaves, lavender oil and the small pouch or bag.

6. Hold the black tourmaline or obsidian crystal in your dominant hand and close your eyes. Visualize a bright white light surrounding you, forming an impenetrable shield against negativity. Feel this shield growing stronger with each breath you take.

7. Now, open your eyes, set down the black tourmaline or obsidian crystal and take the dried rosemary leaves in both hands and rub them together gently. As you do so, imagine any negative energies being absorbed by the herb's purifying properties.

8. Once you feel cleansed, sprinkle some lavender oil onto your palms and rub them together again. Inhale deeply, allowing the calming scent to relax your mind.

9. Place the black tourmaline or obsidian crystal into the pouch along with the dried rosemary leaves. Close your eyes once more and repeat these words:

By Earth's grounding force,
by Air's cleansing breath,
by Fire's protective flame,
and Water's healing flow,
I call upon the energies of the universe
to shield and protect me from all harm.
May this spell empower me with strength and resilience,
Guiding me through life's challenges unharmed.
And so it is.

10. Hold the pouch tightly in your hands, feeling the energy of protection flowing through you. Visualize a bright white light emanating from the

pouch, enveloping you in its warm embrace. Know that this light will repel any negative forces that come your way.

11. When you feel ready, open your eyes and blow out the candle, symbolizing the completion of the spell. Always keep the pouch close to you – in your pocket or under your pillow – as a reminder of your protected state.

+ ˙ ₊⁺ ✶ ˙ ₊ ˙ ₊ ˙ ✳ ˙ ₊ ⁺ ˙ ₊✶₊˙ ˙ ⁺

Remember, this spell is not a substitute for common sense precautions or professional help when needed. It is merely a tool to enhance your protective energy and build your inner strength and resilience. By regularly practising this spell, you can navigate life's challenges with confidence and security.

The Importance of Self-Care

As well as consciously raising your frequency, practising self-care is vital in calling back your power and achieving a state of harmony that promotes optimal health. Self-care involves nurturing yourself physically, emotionally, mentally and spiritually. Engage in regular mindful practices, create boundaries around work–life balance and choose activities that bring you joy and relaxation such as exercise, meditation, reading a book or spending time with loved ones.

Think about weaving self-care into your morning routine. For me, starting my day with a cup of coffee in bed alongside my dog, Walter, brings me comfort and warmth. It's a moment of tranquillity that prepares me for what lies ahead. Moving into my sacred space, I light candles and engage in smoke cleansing to purify both my physical and spiritual being. This ritual helps me release any negative energy and create an atmosphere conducive to inner reflection. Journaling is another essential part of my morning routine as it allows me to unload any thoughts or emotions that may be weighing on me. This practice helps clear my mind and provides a fresh perspective on life. This is not just about following a set of rituals, but rather about setting the tone for the rest of the day. It allows me to prioritize self-care and establish a sense of peace and clarity before diving into my daily responsibilities.

If you can similarly prioritize self-care as an essential part of your morning routine, you will notice a significant shift in your energy levels and overall wellbeing. Remember that taking care of your mind and body is not selfish; it is essential for leading a healthier life filled with joy, love, peace and abundance.

Connecting to Your Intuition and Psychic Gifts

We touched on how our bodies possess an innate wisdom that communicates with us through sensations and our intuition in Chapter 2. Now you are firmly on the path to coming back to yourself, it's time to delve deeper into connecting with your intuition, as well your psychic gifts.

How to Deepen Your Connection with Your Intuition

We all have intuition because, in simple terms, it is our soul. The gut feeling and the quick decision-making is our soul communicating to us. When this area is aligned and balanced, we can tap into its wisdom and trust its guidance. It serves as a compass, directing us towards choices that align with our true selves.

However, in today's world infused with external distractions and superficial ideals, many of us have lost touch with this profound connection between body and spirit. Connecting with your intuition allows for a deep sense of fulfilment, a realization that there is something greater at play beyond material possessions or societal expectations.

> *When our gut becomes clouded*
> *by stress or imbalance, its signals*
> *may be distorted or ignored.*

We've already explored how incorporating moments of pause, in the form of meditation or deep breathing, into your day can help to reduce stress and enable you to tap into those gut feelings. Journaling is also an effective way to listen to your intuition.

CONNECT DEEPLY WITH YOUR INTUITION JOURNAL PROMPTS

Below are some journal prompts to help you connect more deeply with your intuition. You might find it helpful to keep a record of what your intuition has guided you with to look back on. This helps increase trust and confidence in your intuition and yourself. Before you begin journaling, light a candle and some incense, close your eyes and take three deep breaths. Open your eyes and write out these three questions:

- ❭ What do I need to know right now?

- ❭ What is this feeling here to teach me?

> How can I feel more peace right now in this moment?

Then, connecting to your breath, begin to write anything and everything that comes to mind. Don't judge it; just write it down and keep writing. Once you have finished writing, have a read through and feel the wisdom you have created and connected with.

+ ˙ ₊ ✳ ˙ ₊ ˙ ✴ ˙ ₊ ˙ ✳ ₊ ˙ ₊

Your Psychic Gifts

Your psychic gifts, such as the 'four clairs' senses, are deeply intertwined with intuition, serving as extensions of your innate intuitive abilities. While intuition acts as your inner guidance system, psychic gifts amplify and refine this connection, allowing you to perceive information beyond the physical realm. In essence, psychic gifts and intuition are interconnected facets of your spiritual awareness, working together to provide insights, guidance and understanding from a higher perspective.

Clairvoyance: Seeing What Cannot be Seen by the Human Eye

Clairvoyance refers to psychic seeing. Very often, this comes across as a sort of screen that pops up before you in your mind's eye to provide messages in the form of pictures and symbols. In my experience, it is like a black cinema screen that will show a visual of a person with distinct characteristics or a warning of a future scenario.

Clairaudience: Hearing What Cannot be Heard by the Human Ear

Clairaudience is the ability to hear psychic messages. These may be external, coming from a source outside your head, or internal, coming from a voice in your head. Clairaudience is when inspiration and creativity come naturally and suddenly to you. If you're often inspired out of the blue, with ideas popping into your head as though someone said them aloud, you may be tapped into clairaudience. I experience this as words popping into my head and coming through unfiltered.

Another form of clairaudience is when during your childhood you may have had an imaginary friend you talked to. This friend may have been a spirit guide appearing in a form that made sense to you (*we'll explore spirit guides and their role in our life in Chapter 13*).

Claircognizance: Clearly Knowing Without Needing to Use the Physical Mind

Claircognizance is really all about having intense gut feelings and using that information to guide you. For instance, I use my claircognizance in my Guidance Medicine Readings® to decode messages from spirits or beings I am connecting with. Doing this allows me to tap into the energy of a situation or individual, and 'energetically download' information about their past, present or future.

One of the most common signs that you might have claircognizant abilities is the tendency to have sudden insights or ideas. These can also be called 'downloads' – you've probably heard this term on social media. These insights might come to you seemingly out of nowhere. You might get flashes of inspiration or strong gut feelings about a course of action or a particular situation. You might get downloads of information, also seemingly out of nowhere, that suddenly help you.

Clairsentience: Feeling the Feelings of Others

Clairsentience is a tactile psychic feeling. It involves perceiving intuitive insights through physical sensations or emotions. When you start to tap into this ability, you will empathize deeply with others' emotions and sense energies in their surroundings without any rational explanation.

My clairsentience gift is strong, so I feel overwhelmed in large gatherings of people because I can feel their anger, excitement, concern – or anything else. It's difficult to be around others because switching through so many emotions in such a short space of time can be physically exhausting. It is also how I sense other spiritual beings, whether those hanging out with me or trying to send me a message.

Some other psychic abilities that you have probably heard of are:

Telepathy: the ability to communicate thoughts or ideas without physical means. This is more than simply reading minds, and can also refer to reading moods, experiences and more. Telepathic abilities enable you to act on the will to either absorb information from another through your third eye chakra or solar plexus and throat chakra to the receiver.

Precognition: often referred to as 'future sight', this is a psychic ability that enables individuals to perceive or predict future events before they occur. This intuitive gift allows you to tap into the fabric of time and glimpse potential outcomes or developments that lie ahead. You may experience visions, dreams or intuitive insights that offer glimpses into the unfolding of future events, serving as valuable tools for navigating life's twists and turns with greater foresight and awareness.

Astral projection or astral travelling: also known as an out-of-body experience, this can be brought about on purpose or discovered accidentally. It's an event where the astral body leaves the physical body behind, helping the consciousness to enter higher plains. I have dreams that allow my soul to leave my body temporarily and travel to an environment that can exist in my reality or another dimension. What is beautiful about these abilities is that you do not need to be asleep to access them; they can often be reached through shamanic practices or through meditation. See page 214 for more on this.

Aura reading: in combination with other psychic gifts like empathy, this can be used to identify people from a crowd who need support or spiritual guidance. Once you've spotted someone in need, you can help them work towards solving their problems, correcting their aura. Refer back to pages 131-35 for more on auras.

These occurrences, visions, feelings and premonitions all reveal that you are psychically in tune with the universe. It is important to be mindful of them and not to dismiss them because they often help us engage more fully with one another; and, sometimes, can even warn us of a possible danger ahead.

How to Tap into Your Psychic Abilities

To strengthen clairvoyance, you want to care for your third eye chakra (*see page 129*) and always ensure open energy flow. You can use crystals that resonate with the third eye, like amethyst, during meditation to enhance and recharge your third eye focus. While in meditation practice, you can see what images pop into your mind and send messages. In your journal, write down any visions that came to mind with as much detail as you can detect.

To strengthen clairaudience, you can work on recognizing subtle sounds all around you and write them down. Sitting in stillness and quiet, in nature or a sacred space within your home will help you.

To strengthen clairsentience, your environment is the most important thing. You should frequently smoke-cleanse yourself and your home to protect your aura. You will feel and absorb so many frequencies around you that you want to maintain a grounded balance in your own frequency. Practise detecting the sensations of different objects, also called psychometry, where you hold objects to receive messages or take the energetic temperature of a space. In your journal, write down the sensations and look for patterns over time as to what signs and messages you understood in those moments.

To strengthen claircognizance, you need to convene with your spirit guides and higher beings (*we'll explore these in Chapters 13 and 14*). Recognizing these takes trust, intuition and willingness to traverse other dimensions and realms through your mind and body. Crystals such as pyrite and citrine can assist you. In your journal, write down all the hunches you have along the way, paying special attention to times when you feel like you 'just know' something.

Let Go of Negative Energy

If you want to tap into your psychic powers, it's time to let go of any negativity from your past. You must let go of any grudges that you have with the people around you, especially if that person is a close friend or relative, as this can block your energy from interpreting the messages, dreams or feelings correctly.

Practise Mindful Meditation

To be at one with your psychic abilities, slow things down by practising mindful meditation. Take a few minutes every day to just sit in silence and absorb natural energy. When actively meditating, you will feel your body releasing any negativity and stress that was holding you back.

Create a relaxing environment where you feel comfortable channeling your psychic skills or focusing on your intuition.

Listen to Your Body

A healthy body is the most important step to channeling your psychic powers. Listen to your body and stick to what you are comfortable with. Simple stretches, yoga and daily walks all count as exercise – you don't need to run miles every day to keep your body at its best to connect.

Unlock Psychic Gifts Spell

Harnessing your psychic gifts is an ancient pursuit that continues to intrigue us today. By utilizing spells like this one, you can tap into your inner potential and explore the vast depths of your consciousness. Embrace this magical journey with an open mind and heart; who knows what wonders await those who dare to unlock their psychic gifts?

The perfect time for this spell is: any time during the moon phases, but great as a year closes or during Samhain (*see page 64*).

Tools

For this spell you will need the following items:

> matches

> a cleansing tool such as incense, a smoke wand or resin

> a purple candle – either a dinner candle or a tea light candle is fine

> your journal and a pen

Instructions

1. To begin, find a quiet and peaceful space where you can focus your energy.

2. Smoke-cleanse yourself, your space and the candle.

3. Light the candle, symbolizing spiritual awakening and intuition.

4. Ground yourself. Close your eyes and take several deep breaths, allowing yourself to relax and let go of any distractions.

5. Next, visualize a bright light surrounding you, filling you with positive energy. Imagine this light flowing through your body, awakening your psychic abilities.

6. Repeat the following incantation:

> *By the power within me, I call upon my psychic gifts.*
> *Open my third eye, allow me to see beyond the veil.*
> *Grant me clarity and insight*
> *as I embrace my intuition.*

7. As you recite these words, feel the energy building within you. Visualize your third eye opening wide, revealing new realms of knowledge and understanding.

8. After completing the spell, open your eyes and take some time for reflection in your journal and meditation. Pay attention to any signs or messages that may come your way in the following days or weeks.

+ ˙ ₊ ✳ ˙ + ˙ ˙ ✳ ˙ ₊ ˙ ✳ ₊ ˙ ˙ +

These techniques enable you to break free from the clutches of past regrets or future anxieties, allowing you to fully immerse yourself in the beauty and richness of every fleeting moment, creating a deeper awareness of self and opening the path to calling back your power.

When in the present moment, it is there that you can also connect to the other dimensions around and within you. This connects you to your soul and allows space for your psychic abilities to work. It's time for you to step into the higher dimensions.

PART IV

Seeking Guidance from Higher Dimensions

Over the years, I have delved deep into the realms of different dimensions and beings, and it has been an exhilarating journey. Through my personal experiences, I have come to realize that we all possess the innate ability to tap into these dimensions and receive guidance from them.

Working with different dimensions will open up a whole new world of possibilities for you. It will allow you to expand your consciousness beyond the limitations of your physical existence and connect with higher realms of knowledge and wisdom. These dimensions are not bound by time or space, making them a limitless source of information and insight.

When you tap into these dimensions, you can receive guidance on various aspects of life – be it relationships, career choices, personal growth or spiritual development. The insights you gain can help you make informed decisions and navigate through life's challenges more effectively.

However, it is crucial to approach this realm with an open mind and discernment. Not every experience or message will resonate with everyone. What works for one person may not work for another. Therefore, it is essential to take what resonates with you and leave behind what doesn't. Trust the intuition that you have now honed and discern which guidance aligns with your own truth.

CHAPTER 11

The Dimensions

D imensions refer to different planes of existence or levels of consciousness that exist beyond our physical reality. Living as a witch working with dimensions requires a deep understanding of energy and its manipulation. Through meditation and trance-like states, you can transcend the limitations of your three-dimensional world and explore new realms.

Before we explore how to connect to the dimensions through channeling, let's look at the different dimensions that are beyond our selves and the earthly realm.

1D. Earth – the soil, mushrooms, plants and minerals; the elements of earth, water, fire and air. I have also connected with/ seen dragons, phoenixes and other 'mythical' creatures in this dimension because of their connections to the energy from this elemental dimension. This is Mother Earth and is a very grounding dimension.

2D. Biological Life and Organic Matter – the trees, plants, fungi, animals and vitamins. As we explored in Chapter 6, plants are spiritually powerful and enlightened beings. Fungi are among the most intelligent species on Earth, acting like a web underneath the trees and plants connecting everything together. This dimension offers us wisdom.

3D. The Physical – our human body; an individual with an ego and a body that is separate from everyone and everything else.

As humans, we currently live in a 3D reality, with us mostly holding a strong awareness of our being an individual that is separate from everyone and everything else. That is, until we have a spiritual awakening, which can come from a deep self-awareness, usually through the experience of positive and negative polarities and psychological suffering.

Prior to our Earth incarnation, we select a particular set of interactions to experience as our life's mission. That is our life purpose. Karma is the set of geometries that we did not fully experience in our last life, and which we then are carrying over into our next incarnation. The concept of reincarnation has been deeply ingrained in various cultures and religions throughout history. It suggests that our souls are not confined to a single lifetime, but instead undergo a continuous cycle of birth, death and rebirth.

4D. Energy Centres – the energy centres within, also known as our astral body, energy body, light body, emotional body and etheric body.

The energy centres within the body are called the seven chakras (*see page 120*). This dimension deals with our connection to something greater than ourselves, such as a higher power or universal consciousness, expanding beyond what we know as our physical reality and turning more towards our non-physical, spiritual realities. It allows us to explore concepts such as faith, intuition and transcendence.

5D. The Casual Plane – the astral plane or subtle body. This is the bridge between the physical and spiritual realms, connecting us to higher levels of consciousness. This etheric dimension offers a deeper understanding of our existence and connection to the universe. It allows us to tap into our intuition, creativity and spiritual growth. By exploring this realm, we can expand our consciousness and connect with a higher power beyond ourselves. Unconditional love and non-judgement are key characteristics of 5D.

6D. The Universe Itself and Extra-Terrestrial Races – the law of attraction asserts that like attracts like, and that the energy you emit into the world will be mirrored back to you. This principle extends beyond Earth, suggesting that humanity's collective consciousness can influence cosmic forces and potentially attract interactions with extra-terrestrial beings. By aligning thoughts, emotions and actions with positive intentions, individuals may manifest desired outcomes in their lives, while also potentially influencing encounters with extra-terrestrial races based on the vibrational frequency of humanity's collective consciousness.

The universe also responds to us in many ways – it is working with, not against, us. Even events that might not at first seem to be related to each other are indicators that the universe is working with us. They can seem like random occurrences, things that are the result of coincidence. If we look at these more closely, though, they can show us that the universe is listening to us and communicating with us. Things have happened throughout my life for a reason, even when that reason wasn't clear to me at the time. These events are what are known as signs and synchronicities from the universe.

Signs from the Universe – signs from the universe are any event or object that holds a significance or meaning to an individual. These can come in many forms, such as a particular animal appearing across someone's path, or repeatedly in their daily life (*as we explored on page 108*), seeing the same number sequence repeatedly (such as 11:11 or 222) or a dream that seems to hold important information. A sign can even be a chance encounter with someone who provides valuable insight through a beautiful conversation. It's hard to dismiss this as random chance!

Synchronicities are events that seem to be connected in some way despite having no relationship to them. For example, you might be thinking about an old friend you haven't seen in years when suddenly they call you out of the blue.

These signs and synchronicities from the universe are sent to guide us on our path or provide answers to questions we may have been struggling with. By paying attention to these messages from the universe, we can gain insight into our true path and make decisions that align with our soul's purpose. Being open to these signs also means that we gain an awareness that our lives are filled with both positive and negative events, that nothing is better or worse. No matter what occurs in your life, whether positive or negative, there is a purpose behind it. By harnessing that energy, you can transform even undesirable situations into ones you prefer.

ℛECEIVE GUIDANCE FROM THE UNIVERSE JOURNAL PROMPTS

> What patterns or recurring themes do I notice in my life? By regularly reflecting on this question, you may begin to recognize connections between events and circumstances.

> How did I feel when this event occurred? Did it resonate with me on a deeper level? Journaling about your feelings can provide valuable insight into the significance of these synchronicities in your life.

Consider recording any dreams or symbols that appear repeatedly. Dreams often contain hidden messages from the subconscious mind and can offer guidance or warnings about future events. By keeping track of these symbols and their meanings over time, you may uncover valuable information about the synchronicities unfolding around you.

Extra-Terrestrials – are here to help humanity evolve spiritually. They want to assist the ascension of planet Earth by raising the collective consciousness. Aliens use UFOs as their transport. UFOs operate at a very high speed in the higher dimensions and are invisible to us. When the UFOs enter the Earth's vibration, which is very condensed and slow, they become visible. During night-time sky-gazing, I occasionally spot fast-moving UFOs resembling stars, but exhibiting unusual movements. They dart erratically, not moving on a straight path, and then vanish swiftly. These sightings aren't confined to the night; I've also observed balls of light encircling disc-shaped objects during the daytime, only for them to swiftly depart from view.

This may seem far-fetched to some, but, throughout history, countless individuals have reported encounters with beings from other worlds, sharing stories of profound wisdom and spiritual enlightenment. At times, during your dreams or through meditation, you, too, may receive guidance from extra-terrestrials. We'll explore this more thoroughly in Chapter 14.

7D. The Spirit World and Spirit Guides – religious texts refer to this dimension as Heaven. The spirit world exists all around and through the material world that human beings inhabit, but in a different dimension. Spirits are individuals who have passed away and transitioned to the spirit world. A 'spirit guide' typically refers to a spirit who has spent considerable time in the spirit world, acquiring the knowledge and skills needed to guide others. They may also be an ancestor with a connection from a past life or simply a spirit drawn to events along your life path, recognizing their ability to offer assistance.

One of the most significant benefits of working with the spirit world dimension is gaining access to ancient wisdom and knowledge that has been passed down through generations. In this dimension, you can seek guidance from spirits who have lived before you and possess vast knowledge about various aspects of life. By establishing a connection with these spirits, you can tap into their wisdom and learn valuable lessons. You'll learn how to connect to the spirit world and your spirit guide in Chapters 12 and 13.

8D. The Ascended Masters – a group of highly evolved spiritual beings who have transcended the cycle of birth and death. They have achieved a state of enlightenment and mastery over the physical world and are guiding humanity towards its ultimate spiritual evolution. These masters have lived on Earth in the past and have left behind teachings that continue to inspire people today. Some of the most well-known ascended masters include Jesus Christ, Buddha, Krishna and Saint Germain. They can be contacted directly through meditation or prayer – we'll explore this further in Chapter 14. Some people claim to have received messages or visions from these enlightened beings. They offer guidance and support to those who seek their help in achieving greater levels of consciousness.

9D. Angels – beings of divine light and love, play a significant role in our lives, offering guidance, protection, comfort and healing. They are spiritual entities that serve as messengers and guardians, guiding us along our life paths and supporting us through challenges. Whether through subtle nudges, synchronicities or profound encounters, angels communicate with us in various ways, reminding us of our inner strength and connection to the divine. Their presence brings reassurance in times of uncertainty, offering solace and encouragement as we navigate the complexities of existence. Angels are compassionate companions on our journey, shining their luminous presence to illuminate our paths and infuse our lives with divine grace and blessings.

10D. Archangels – revered as the highest-ranking angels in the celestial hierarchy, possess immense power and wisdom that transcend the bounds of the earthly realm. Serving as divine messengers and guardians, they offer guidance, protection and support to humanity, assisting us in connecting with our higher selves and accessing our inner wisdom. Through their benevolent presence and unwavering light, archangels illuminate the path to spiritual enlightenment and self-discovery, empowering us to transcend limitations and embrace our true potential. By invoking the assistance of archangels, we can cultivate a deeper connection to the divine and awaken the dormant wisdom within, allowing us to navigate life's challenges with grace, clarity and divine guidance. We'll explore how to connect to these higher-dimensional beings in Chapter 14.

11D. The Akashic Records – this dimension can provide valuable insights into our past lives, present circumstances and future possibilities. 'The Akashic Records' refers to a cosmic library that contains all the information about every soul and its journey through time and space. It is within this cosmic library where the 'Council of 12' are.

The Council is a collective of 12 tall light beings who guard everyone's soul's contracts in the library. They are here to assist with the Earth's accession and help humanity. I would like to share a personal experience I have had with the Council.

In 2019, after the loss of my father and my mother telling me she had cancer, I discovered how I can help others. I remember taking myself off into nature to clear my head. I walked into a huge cornfield and sat down within the corn. The corn was so high it towered over my head. I sat and connected back to self and then all the fear came rushing into my mind about my family. I placed my hand on my heart and asked the universe, 'What do you want me to do?' It was in that exact moment I met the Council. Being so used to connecting to the spirit world and spirit guides, this felt very different. I could see 12 tall beings that looked like light. They all harmoniously communicated telepathically to me. They showed me how I work and how I tap into the different dimensions. They told me I was meant to do something called 'Guidance Medicine Readings'. These would consist of one-on-one sessions combining my knowledge as a witch and my own spiritual practice. I was to be of service and use everything I had learned throughout my life to help others. As always, I surrendered to full trust. The Council has continued to work with me daily.

12D. The Source – this is the dimension of God Consciousness and transcends conventional understandings of reality, encompassing the essence of Source within every particle and entity across all dimensional planes – from the foundational 1D to the expansive realms beyond.

Here, the divine essence permeates the fabric of existence, infusing every aspect of creation with its boundless light and wisdom. Referred to by some beings and spirits as 'pure light' or 'the one', this dimension represents the highest expression of spiritual awareness and unity consciousness.

As an intuitive channeler, I traverse the various dimensions, from 4D to 12D. My work involves a blend of energies spanning different dimensions:

1. The universe: collaborating with me through visual synchronicities, tests, challenges and the manifestation of my intentions.

2. Intuition: a soft, gentle inner knowing emanating from the depths of my soul within my heart space.

3. Downloads: channeling messages from the Council of 12, tapping into wisdom beyond the earthly realm.

Connecting with other dimensions may seem like a practice reserved for mystics and spiritual seekers, and society often discourages us from exploring this realm, dismissing it as mere imagination or superstition. However, it is an innate ability we all possess and is accessible to anyone who has an open mind and a willingness to explore beyond what is immediately apparent in our physical reality.

You, too, have access to all these dimensions of consciousness at any moment and place. Tapping into these dimensions just requires practice and discipline through meditation and mindfulness practices such as journaling.

*By honing your skills and cultivating trust
in your abilities, you can tap into profound
wisdom beyond this physical realm.*

Channeling offers another opportunity for connection with spiritual energies that can bring insight, healing, creativity and transformation into your life journey.

Connecting to the Dimensions through Channeling

Channeling is the process of receiving and transmitting information from a source beyond our physical realm. It allows you to communicate with entities or energies from higher dimensions, offering profound wisdom and guidance.

In understanding what channeling entails, it is essential to recognize that it is not confined to any particular belief system or religious doctrine. Rather, channeling represents a universal pursuit of connecting with higher consciousness or divine sources. By opening yourself up as a channel, you will receive messages or information from spiritual guides, ascended masters, angels or even loved ones in the spirit world.

To begin your exploration of channeling, it is essential to understand that we are all energetic beings connected to a vast universal consciousness. Channeling allows us to tap into this collective energy and access information beyond our limited human perspective. The first step in developing channeling abilities is cultivating a deep sense of self-awareness and inner stillness through meditation. This state of inner stillness creates a fertile ground for receiving messages from spiritual entities.

When engaging in any form of channeling, it is crucial to establish clear boundaries and protection mechanisms. Opening yourself up energetically can leave you vulnerable to negative or lower vibrational entities. Setting the intention to connect only with beings of love and light, as well as visualizing a protective shield of white light around yourself (*see the protection spell on page 155*), can help maintain a safe and positive channeling experience.

Channeling involves consciously shifting your mind and mental space to achieve an expanded state of consciousness. Channeling enables me to access and convey profound insights and guidance from the higher realms, including communicating with one's higher self, the archangels, ascended masters, star beings, deceased loved ones, spiritual deities, nature spirits, fairies and spiritual guides. It is how I communicate to the Council of 12 in 11D. It involves me raising my vibration by opening my heart chakra to connect with the Council directly. During conscious channeling, I am in a relaxed and expanded state of consciousness that occurs when they allow higher vibrational beings to align with them for the purpose of communication, healing and the sharing of information.

When I channel, I set my own thoughts aside to make room for the messages to arrive, translating messages from beings that exist outside of the 3D reality. My job is just to relay what I am sensing, with no doubt. I have simply vibrationally elevated so that I become a frequency match for the Council. The conscious channelled message is like a stream of consciousness alongside my own. I receive the message word for word and pass it on directly to my clients. The Council shows me warnings by showing me neon signs, or symbols such as roses, which I know means love. They appear like little movies in my mind that I relay to my clients. When a client or anyone asks me a question, that is my trigger, my 'on switch', to receive information from the Council. I relay what I hear, see and feel. I can even pause, ask for clarification or stop the message and connection. When I quiet my mind, open my heart and tune into this frequency through channeling, I am shifting away from the doubt and ego, into the clarity of love.

Through this practice, I have gained profound insights into my life's purpose and those of others. While sceptics may dismiss channeling as mere fantasy or delusion, those who have experienced its transformative power understand its potential for unlocking hidden truths within us and connecting with higher realms of consciousness.

How to Channel to a Higher Dimension

Witches often use tools such as crystals and herbs to channel their energy and open portals to other dimensions. By incorporating herbs into their practices through burning, brewing or scattering, witches can infuse their magic with the elemental energies of the plant kingdom. Different herbs are chosen for their specific magical correspondences, such as protection, healing or manifestation, allowing witches to align their intentions with the energies of nature.

Witches also select specific crystals based on their metaphysical properties and intentions when channeling. By meditating with or wearing crystals, they can attune their energy to the vibrations of the stones, amplifying their magical intentions and enhancing spiritual connections. Crystals act as conduits for channeling energy, helping to focus intentions and access higher realms of consciousness.

Another way witches can channel energy is through the use of spoken or written incantations to invoke and direct energy towards their desired outcomes. Through the power of words, witches can focus their intentions, raise energy and communicate with the unseen realms. By crafting and reciting incantations with clear intent and conviction, witches can strengthen their magical workings and create shifts in consciousness, opening doorways to other dimensions and inviting spiritual guidance and assistance.

As a witch, you, too, can harness the potent energies of crystals and herbs to facilitate your magical workings and open portals to other dimensions. See pages 45 and 97 for guidance on which herbs and crystals to use. We'll explore how to connect to higher-dimensional beings through incantation on page 212.

Below is a further exercise to help you channel to a higher dimension. Once you have completed it, I recommend you journal about your experience. In order to tap into the vast potential of your mind and connect with a higher level of consciousness, it is essential to cultivate a sense of mindfulness and inner awareness. This exercise will guide you towards this state of being.

CHANNEL TO A HIGHER DIMENSION MEDITATION

❭ Begin by finding a quiet and comfortable space where you can sit or lie down without any distractions. Close your eyes and take a few deep breaths, allowing yourself to relax and let go of any tension in your body.

❭ Now, bring your attention to the present moment by focusing on your breath. Feel the sensation of each inhale and exhale, noticing how the air enters and leaves your body. As thoughts arise, acknowledge them without judgement and gently bring your focus back to your breath.

❭ Next, imagine yourself surrounded by a radiant light that represents pure positive energy. Visualize this light entering through the top of your head, filling every cell in your body with its healing power. Feel its warmth spreading through you, dissolving any negativity or blockages within.

❭ As you continue breathing deeply, expand this light beyond yourself into the world around you. Envision it reaching outwards, connecting with all living beings and radiating love and compassion towards them.

❭ Now, shift your attention inward once again and imagine stepping into a lift that will transport you to a higher dimension. As the doors close behind you, feel yourself ascending effortlessly towards this elevated state of consciousness.

❭ As the lift reaches its destination, allow yourself to fully immerse in this new dimension. Notice how everything feels lighter, clearer and more vibrant here. Take some time to explore this realm; observe its beauty and wisdom as it unfolds before you.

❭ When you are ready to return from this higher dimension, step back into the lift and press the button for descent. Feel yourself gradually descending back into ordinary reality while carrying with you everything you have experienced.

Once you have completed this exercise and established a regular **meditation** practice, you can begin exploring different **techniques** for channeling, which I've touched on below. Automatic writing can be practised alone, while the others would usually be taught by a practitioner. Each approach offers its own unique set of experiences and possibilities.

Automatic Writing

Automatic writing is a channeling method where you allow your hand to move freely across paper without conscious control. This process often results in written messages from spiritual guides or entities. With practice, you can learn to essentially 'turn down' the volume of your conscious thoughts while allowing higher guidance to come through you as you write. As you begin to trust yourself more and more, it can feel like you're just making it up in your head – know that that is part of the process.

Trance Mediumship

Trance mediumship involves entering an altered state of consciousness where the practitioner allows their body to be used as a vessel for spirit communication. During trance mediumship sessions, your conscious mind steps aside while allowing another entity or guide to speak through you.

Physical Mediumship

Physical mediumship involves the communication of spirit entities or energies through a physical medium. In this form of mediumship, the medium's body serves as a conduit for the transmission of messages or manifestations from the spirit world. Physical phenomena such as direct voice, trance speaking, table tipping and ectoplasmic manifestations are commonly associated with physical mediumship. The medium enters into an altered state of consciousness, allowing spirit entities to temporarily control or manipulate their physical body to convey messages or perform phenomena. Physical mediumship requires rigorous development and training, and often occurs in a controlled environment with experienced sitters or observers present to witness and document the phenomena. Physical mediumship provides a direct link between the spirit world and the physical realm, offering insights, healing and evidence of life beyond the material plane.

Mental Mediumship

Channeling through mental mediumship involves the communication of spiritual information, messages or insights from the spirit world through the medium's mind. Unlike physical mediumship, where the medium's body serves as a conduit, mental mediumship primarily utilizes the medium's mental faculties, such as clairvoyance, clairaudience, clairsentience and intuition, to receive and interpret messages from spirit entities. The medium may receive impressions, images, words or feelings from the spirit world, which they then convey to the recipient or sitter. Mental mediumship sessions often involve the medium entering a focused or altered state of consciousness, such as a light trance or heightened awareness, to facilitate clearer communication with spirit entities.

Channeling through Energy Healing

This involves the transmission of healing energy from the practitioner to the recipient for the purpose of restoring balance, harmony and vitality to the body, mind and spirit. In this form of channeling, the practitioner serves as a channel or conduit for universal life force energy, also known as chi, which flows through them and into the recipient. By channeling this healing energy, practitioners can address energetic blockages, release stagnant or negative energy, and promote the body's natural ability to heal itself. Energy healing modalities such as reiki healing are commonly used to facilitate this process, offering profound benefits for physical, emotional and spiritual wellbeing.

By delving into the understanding of different dimensions, you have broadened your perception and elevated your consciousness.

As you explore the depths of higher awareness, you tap into regions of your brain associated with enhanced self-awareness, empathy and compassion, fostering a shift from fear to love in your actions and perspectives. Embracing this expanded consciousness dissolves the barriers of isolation and fear, and allows you to recognize the interconnectedness of all existence and the ever-present support and love surrounding you.

The chapters that follow are dedicated to the spirit world, spirit guides, ascended masters, angels, extra-terrestrials and the Council, so you can focus on those spiritual entities and energies that will directly interact with and guide you on your journey. Through understanding and connecting with these spiritual beings, you will unlock deeper layers of wisdom and spiritual growth.

CHAPTER 12

The Spirit World

Part of returning home to self is to use the wisdom from your ancestors and to feel a deep bond with the spirits that you connect with. These spirits are your allies and co-creators in your magical journey. This connection fosters a sense of belonging and purpose, allowing you to embrace your true nature and step into your power.

Our loved ones who have safely transitioned to the spirit world can communicate with us in different ways. Before we explore how to connect with the spirit world, I first want to explain about death. There is no death; everything is energy, so when you die your soul just transcends out of the body into another dimension. Loved ones in the spirit world can come to us through dreams, scents, telepathically and even through songs, signs or seemingly serendipitous events. Yes, they can move stuff, but their energy will be soft, loving and light. Generally, you will feel safe with their presence. When I mention spirits, people jump to the word ghost. Having worked with spirits for a long time now, I have learned that there is a big difference between communicating with someone who is in the spirit world versus communicating with a ghost. Ghosts do not know they are dead – they have missed their opening to go to the spirit world and are stuck between realms. A traumatic death or unfinished business keeps them stuck on the Earth plane. Ghosts are distressed, confused and lost. They know you can feel them, and your fear feeds their energy. There are some darker spirits out there, but you can protect yourself through your own vibrational power and light. See page 34 for a White Light Protection Spell, and page 155 for a Witch's Protection Spell for Oneself.

So, what is it like in the spirit world? The spirit world is not limited to one specific location, but rather exists alongside our physical reality. During my journey, I have connected to many spirits from the spirit world, and they have all said the same to me: that spirits are all around us, coexisting in an invisible dimension. When you die, the soul enters a state of eternal bliss. Some spirits have shared with me their encounters with beings of light who guide them through a tunnel or towards a bright light. Some even claim to have had a life review, where they relive significant moments of their lives and experience the emotions of those they affected. In the spirit world dimension, they are free from pain, suffering and all earthly desires. It is described as a place of pure love and light, where souls can reunite with their loved ones who have passed away before them.

I'm often asked what communicating with a spirit looks and feels like. It's hard to describe, but spirit messages manifest in your mind using your own voice. However, when you pose questions, the spirit responds immediately. Your 'human mind' simply could not reply that swiftly. I work with all the senses, so I see spirits as a form, which is usually fleeting and quick. When I am connecting, I see spirits in my third eye (*see page 129*), like replaying a movie in my mind. When I am channeling for someone, I work with my spirit Council of 12 and my client's spirit guide (we'll explore spirit guides in the next chapter). I see them, feel them and hear them, and have a three-way conversation.

Your spiritual team consists of your ancestors and loved ones who have passed over into the spirit world and your spirit guides. Everyone has this spiritual team, who are with you your whole life, guiding you, protecting you and helping you.

Your loved ones are always with you.

Connecting to the Spirit World

Everyone can pick up guidance and information from the spirit world. If you lean into that and believe, then you will receive. It should feel like home. Just tap into the light within you and to the universe – we were born with these abilities; it is part of who we are, we were just taught to forget them. So, trust and believe what you are experiencing and lean in to allow the flow. The gift of talking to spirits is like a muscle: the more you practise, the stronger it gets.

Connecting with the spirit world is much like tuning in to a radio frequency. When tuning into the spirit world you will be raising your frequency.

Before we go any further, there are three 'rules':

1. This is a journey, and it is unique for everyone.

2. Trust what comes, trust what you see. What you receive always holds a meaning.

3. Always ask for protection and for spirits to come forward for the highest good, love and light.

Connecting with the spirit world provides you with guidance, wisdom and comfort. However, for those who have never experienced this type of connection before, it can be difficult to know where to start. If this is you, the steps below should ease you in.

HOW TO CONNECT TO A SPIRIT IN THE SPIRIT WORLD

The first step before you start to connect is to create a space that you feel comfortable in to open yourself up to receiving messages. Sit on a chair or cross-legged on the floor. If you like, light a candle or use aromatherapy. The reason you're doing this is not to bring the spirit closer to you. Spirits do not care what candles you light or what chair you sit in. You are setting the stage for you, not the spirit. This is helping you to physically set the intention.

Once you've created your space, close your eyes and breathe deeply. You are ready to start your connection.

1. Protection: visualize a white light around you or a bubble of protection (see page 34).

2. Set your intention: state in your mind your intention to open a door in your mind to speak to and receive messages from the spirit world.

3. Meditation: connect to your breath in your heart space.

4. Blank your mind: the blank reading screen is your viewing space – it is where you will receive images and pictures through which the spirit may communicate. Using your mind's eye, imagine a large movie screen in front of you. When you have held this screen in your mind and there is nothing else in your mind other than black stillness, NOW is the time to ASK. Ask your question. Or ask for a message from the spirit. Don't demand, just ask. Let the answer come. When you feel there is nothing left, connect to your breath and open your eyes. Journal what you experienced.

5. Clearing yourself: Imagine all the cords and energy streams that you were plugged into are being cut. As those are cut, they disconnect you from the unwanted energy. The energy you will feel will be just yours now. Slowly come back into your space. Return to your body. Know that you are in control. When you're ready, the space will be just yours again. Burn a sacred smoke or have a shower or bath to close down your energy.

+ ·,+ ✳ ·,+ ·✳· + ·,✳,+· +

You can also work with tools such as tarot cards or pendulums, which can help you tap into your intuition and receive messages from the spirit world more easily. Tarot cards can be used for divination purposes while pendulums are used to answer yes-or-no questions. When using these tools, it is important to approach them with an open mind and heart.

Spirits communicate through tarot cards by influencing the reader's intuition and interpretation of the cards. It's believed that spirits guide the reader to select specific cards or symbols that hold significance to the question or situation. Through the reader's intuitive abilities and understanding of the tarot symbolism, the spirits convey messages and insights that provide guidance and clarity to the querent. The synchronicity between the cards drawn and the querent's circumstances is often seen as evidence of spiritual communication through the tarot.

Spirit messages can also come through a pendulum by influencing its movements in response to questions or intentions. When using a pendulum, you hold it steady and ask yes-or-no questions or set intentions. Spirits influence the subtle movements of the pendulum, causing it to swing or rotate in specific directions that indicate affirmative or negative responses. The individual's connection to their intuition plays a significant role in interpreting these movements and understanding the messages being conveyed by the spirit realm through the pendulum's motions.

Honouring a Loved One in the Spirit World

Offering prayers and rituals for the departed is a profound way to pay homage to our loved ones who have transcended into the spirit world. It is an age-old tradition that holds deep cultural significance and spiritual importance across various belief systems. These ancient practices provide solace, comfort and a sense of connection with those who have passed away, as we seek to honour their memory in a manner that transcends the physical realm.

One way to honour your loved one in the spirit world is by lighting candles in remembrance of them. The flickering flame represents the eternal light that guides their souls in the afterlife, illuminating their path towards spiritual enlightenment. As you ignite these flames, offer your heartfelt prayers for their wellbeing and peace. The mesmerizing dance of light and shadows creates an ethereal ambience, evoking a mystic union between your world and the spirit realm. This sacred moment provides you with an opportunity for reflection, healing and acceptance of loss. Through prayers and rituals for the departed, like the one below, you can acknowledge that death is not an end, but rather a continuation of life in another form.

CONNECT TO THE SPIRIT WORLD RITUAL

This ritual is a powerful tool for those seeking a deeper understanding of themselves and their place in the universe. This is an ancient practice that has been passed down through many generations. It involves creating a sacred space where you can commune with spirits and seek their wisdom, preferably outdoors where nature's energy can enhance the experience.

The perfect time for this ritual is: full, waning or supermoon, or on a loved one's birthday as a remembrance.

TOOLS

For this ritual you will need the following items:

> four white candles

> four crystals (I recommend using rose quartz and amethyst)

> any mementos that represent your loved ones who are in the spirit world

> photographs of your loved ones who are in the spirit world

> matches

> incense sticks or cones to burn

> your journal and a pen

INSTRUCTIONS

1. Once you have gathered your materials, find a comfortable spot in nature where you can sit undisturbed.

2. Begin by placing your four candles and crystals to represent each cardinal direction – north, south, east and west – symbolizing the four elements: earth, fire, air and water.

3. Place any photographs or mementos of your loved one in the middle.

4. Next, light the candles to create a sacred circle within which you will perform your ritual.

5. Then, light the incense to purify the space and cleanse your energy field. As the smoke rises into the air like ethereal tendrils reaching towards heaven itself, take deep breaths and allow yourself to relax into a state of heightened awareness.

6. With your mind clear and focused on your intention – whether that is seeking guidance or simply connecting with loved ones who have passed on – close your eyes and envision a white light surrounding you. This light serves as protection against any negative energies that may try to interfere with your connection.

7. Now is the time for meditation. Allow yourself to enter a deep state of relaxation while remaining aware of your surroundings. Focus on your breath as it flows in and out, grounding yourself in the present moment. As you do so, imagine a bridge forming between the physical world and the spirit realm.

8. Once you feel connected to this ethereal bridge, begin to call upon the spirits you wish to connect with. Speak their names aloud or silently in your mind, inviting them into your sacred space. Be patient and open-minded as you wait for their presence to manifest.

9. During this time of connection, it is important to remain respectful and humble. Remember that spirits are beings of higher consciousness and should be treated with reverence. Ask your questions or seek guidance from a place of sincerity and gratitude.

10. When you feel ready to conclude the ritual, thank the spirits for their presence and guidance. Open your eyes and blow out the candles one by one, starting from east to west, symbolizing closure of the sacred circle.

11. As you leave your sacred space, take a moment to reflect on your experience. Journaling about any insights or messages received can help solidify your connection with the spirit world.

Now you have learned about the spirit world, it is time to discover your spirit guide. While both spirits and spirit guides belong to the spiritual realm, they differ in their nature, purpose and relationship with humans.

CHAPTER 13

Your Spirit Guide

In the last chapter, you learned that spirits are the souls of deceased individuals who may interact with the living for various reasons. Spirit guides, on the other hand, are non-human entities that offer ongoing guidance and support throughout your life.

We all have spirit guides. They are spiritual beings of the highest truth working on our behalf to guide our thoughts and energy. These beings come in many forms and have different purposes, but their common goal is to help guide us back into alignment with the love of the universe. They are beings that are assigned to us before we are born that help nudge and guide us through life.

Your spirit guides may have been connected to you from a past life – from reincarnation when our souls are reborn into new bodies after death, carrying with them the knowledge and experiences accumulated over multiple lifetimes.

Some of the souls we have encountered in previous incarnations may have chosen to continue their journey alongside us, guiding and supporting us from the spiritual realm. This notion adds depth and complexity to the relationship between ourselves and our spirit guides. It suggests a profound connection rooted in shared experiences across lifetimes. Our spirit guides may possess an intimate understanding of who we are at a soul level because they have walked beside us before.

Some spirit guides will stay with you throughout your entire life, while others will pop in every now and again to help you with specific areas of your life or goals you are trying to achieve. These guides are at varying levels of consciousness themselves. Some may be highly ascended masters (such as Jesus) and others may be your average spirit who just happens to be a master in a certain area. They may appear to have a male or female energy, though, in reality, they are just energy. They may be spirits who have had physical incarnations or they may have never taken corporeal form. You may be the only person they are guiding or they may be on the 'panel' for other people as well.

Before we move into more of who your spirit guides could be, I would like to share a spell to help you connect to a past life of yours. Whether you believe in reincarnation or not, by delving into past lives through a spell like this, regression therapy, meditation or other spiritual practices, you can uncover patterns, traumas and connections that may be influencing your current life. This deeper understanding allows you to release old wounds, heal unresolved issues and gain insights into your soul's journey across multiple lifetimes.

Connect to a Past Life Spell

Connecting with your past lives can provide you with valuable insights into your current existence. By engaging in rituals such as this spell, you open yourself up to new possibilities and expand your understanding of who you are at your core.

The perfect time for this spell is: anytime.

Tools

For this spell you will need the following items:

- matches
- a candle
- items that hold personal significance for you, such as an old photograph or piece of jewellery – anything that evokes a sense of nostalgia or connection to your past

Instructions

1. To embark on this journey of self-discovery, find a quiet and comfortable space where you can focus your energy without distractions.

2. Begin by lighting the candle and placing it in front of you. As you watch the flame flicker and dance, take several deep breaths to centre yourself and clear your mind.

3. Next, gather your personal items. Place these objects around the candle, creating a sacred space for your exploration.

4. Now, close your eyes and visualize yourself standing at the entrance to an ancient temple. Feel the cool stone beneath your feet as you step inside.

5. In one corner of the room lies an ornate wooden chest adorned with intricate carvings. Approach it slowly and open it with reverence. Inside, find a small vial containing fragrant herbs – lavender for relaxation and clarity; rosemary for memory enhancement; and chamomile for soothing energy.

6. Take these herbs in your hands and deeply breathe in their aroma. Allow their scents to transport you back in time – back to another era when you walked this Earth under different circumstances.

7. With each inhale, feel the veil between your present and past lives growing thinner. As you exhale, release any doubts or scepticism that may be holding you back from fully embracing this experience.

8. Now, take a pinch of each herb and sprinkle it into a bowl of warm water. Stir the mixture gently with your fingers, infusing it with your intentions to connect with your past life. Visualize the water becoming charged with energy as you focus on your desire to uncover forgotten memories and gain insight into who you once were.

9. Once the mixture is ready, dip your fingertips into the bowl and anoint yourself on your forehead to open your third eye. Feel energy spreading through your body as these ancient energies awaken within you.

10. Sit quietly for a few moments, allowing yourself to relax and enter a meditative state. As thoughts or images arise in your mind's eye, observe them without judgement or attachment. Trust that whatever comes up is meant to.

11. When you feel ready, slowly bring yourself back to the present moment by taking several deep breaths and open your eyes.

12. As you blow out the candle, know that this spell has led you closer to understanding who you truly are.

Discovering Your Assigned Spirit Guides

Spirit guides assigned to you could include any or all of the following:

Main spirit guide – this is the guide that is always present with you. It will be the one with whom you will spend most of your time and have most of your interactions. This guide is similar to a friend. It behaves like a companion, bringing comfort, laughter and joy. It is around to remind you to handle situations with kindness and diplomacy. It will prompt you to take a breath when things go wrong and to be patient with things difficult to change. This guide advises when choices involve your happiness. It is believed that this guide has lived a human life; because of this, it understands all you are experiencing and what the outcomes of decisions may be.

Archangels – these are leaders in the angel world and have a powerful, very large energy, which you may feel in the room when they come in close to you. Each archangel has a specialty of healing and can work with countless humans at once.

Ascended masters – these were once human, like Buddha or Mother Mary, living journeys of deep spiritual growth and influence. They can appear in your dreams with messages, during deep meditations or signs from them can appear in your daily life, such as seeing their own images.

Departed loved ones – these loved ones or family members who've passed on may choose to be one of your spirit guides and actively support you from heaven by helping you in very practical ways, like sending career opportunities or nurturing relationships your way. One of your grandmothers could be an important spirit guide for you, whether you knew her well in life or not. In fact, any human who has passed on might become a spirit guide for you.

Guardian angels – these are yours exclusively, and we each have more than one! They have devoted their lives to helping just you. Call on them anytime for immediate assistance. They love you unconditionally, forever. Remember that angels are nondenominational and work with people of all faiths and spiritual beliefs.

Higher beings/light beings/extra-terrestrials – these beings choose to become your guide and come with so much knowledge and direction for you. They may have known you from past lives and are here to raise your frequency (*see page 149 for more on the self frequency*). Their insight is incredibly advanced and loving, and it carries great depth. They offer concise ways to reach awakening.

Spirit animals – these might be pets you once had that passed away and are now part of your spiritual guidance squad. Spirit animals can also be any animal that has something to teach you. Spirit animals could show up for the first time in a dream, in your garden or on your friend's coffee mug.

> *Connecting to your spirit guide is an*
> *essential aspect of being a witch.*

Connecting to Your Spirit Guides

As a witch, you can harness the natural energies of the universe to manifest your intentions and create positive change. However, sometimes you may feel disconnected or unsure about your magical practices. This is where your spirit guides come in. They possess vast knowledge and experience in the spiritual realm and can offer invaluable guidance on how to amplify your spells or rituals.

By connecting to your spirit guides, you can enhance your magical abilities, gain insight into your path as a witch and receive guidance in navigating life's challenges. For example, if you are struggling with a particular spell or finding it challenging to manifest your desires, you can call upon your spirit guides for assistance. Through meditation or other forms of communication, such as divination tools like tarot cards or pendulums (*see page 195*), you can establish a direct line of communication with them. They may provide insights on how to refine your intentions or suggest alternative approaches that align better with the energies at play.

Connecting with your spirit guides also allows you to gain profound insight into your path as a witch. Every witch has their unique journey in the realm of magic; however, it is not uncommon for us to feel lost or uncertain about our purpose at times. By seeking guidance from your spirit guides, you can gain clarity on your mission and purpose, and receive wisdom and support along your journey of self-discovery and healing. Your spirit guides may reveal hidden talents or gifts that you were unaware of before. They might also provide guidance on which areas of magic you should focus on developing further based on your strengths and interests. This insight not only helps you grow as a witch, but also brings a sense of fulfilment and purpose to your practice.

Lastly, connecting to your spirit guides can provide invaluable guidance in navigating life's challenges. As witches, we face various obstacles and difficulties in our daily lives. Whether it is personal struggles, relationship issues or career dilemmas, our spirit guides can offer wisdom and support during these times.

When faced with a difficult decision or situation, connecting with your spirit guides can offer valuable guidance. Below is a simple daily exercise to connect with your spirit guides.

STEPS TO CONNECT TO YOUR SPIRIT GUIDES

Find a quiet and comfortable space where you won't be disturbed. Sit or lie down in a relaxed position and take a few deep breaths to centre yourself.

1. Begin by setting a clear intention to connect with your spirit guide. You can do this silently or aloud, expressing your desire for their guidance and presence in your life.

2. Close your eyes and visualize a warm, inviting light surrounding you, creating a safe and sacred space for communication with your spirit guide.

3. Focus on your breath, allowing it to become slow and steady. With each inhale, imagine yourself drawing in positive energy and openness. With each exhale, release any tension or doubt.

4. Once you feel centred and grounded, pose a question or simply ask for guidance from your spirit guide. You can speak this aloud or silently in your mind.

5. Trust your intuition and remain open to receiving messages. Pay attention to any thoughts, feelings, images or sensations that come to you. Your spirit guide may communicate with you in various ways, so be receptive to whatever form their guidance takes.

6. Take a few moments to express gratitude for any insights or guidance you've received. Trust that your spirit guide is always with you and available to support you on your journey.

7. When you're ready, gently bring your awareness back to the present moment. Wiggle your fingers and toes, and slowly open your eyes.

8. Afterwards I would recommend you journal about your experience.

$$+ \cdot {}_{+} {}^{+} \ast \cdot {}_{+} \cdot {}_{+} \cdot \overset{\cdot}{\ast} \cdot {}^{+} \cdot {}_{+} \cdot \ast {}_{+} {}^{+} \cdot {}_{+}$$

Alternatively, you may choose to use divination tools such as tarot cards, pendulums or scrying mirrors to seek guidance. Focus on your question or intention and trust that your spirit guides will communicate with you through signs, symbols or intuitive insights revealed during the practice. Embrace patience and openness as you await their guidance, knowing that they are there to support you on your journey.

Your spirit guide can come forward in several ways:

◗ Sending signs: guides can arrange synchronicities to help alert you to something you need to see or know about.

◗ Gut feelings: guides can poke you in the gut when you're experiencing something they want you to pay attention to.

◗ Intuitive insight: guides can send you flashes of intuition which may sound like a voice in your head.

◗ Sending people into your life: your guides sometimes get together with other people's guides and together they try to create a meeting between their charges.

◗ Arranging and nudging: guides can also nudge you in the direction they want you to go or arrange for something to happen to you.

By delving into the spirit world and establishing a connection with your spirit guides, you have unlocked a vast source of knowledge that can assist you in navigating through life's challenges. Remember that building this relationship takes time and patience; it requires consistent practice and an open heart.

Now, let's ascend to connect with higher-dimensional beings who can offer guidance in your life.

CHAPTER 14

Higher-Dimensional Beings

Higher beings – from the ascended masters to the angels to the Council and extra-terrestrials – possess immense knowledge and understanding of the universe beyond our comprehension, offering profound insights that can assist you on your journey home to yourself.

The wisdom of higher-dimensional beings transcends our limited human perspective, providing us with a broader understanding of our purpose and potential in life. Through their guidance, we can tap into a higher dimension where we receive downloads of information and profound wisdom that can shape our path back to ourselves.

It is through this connection that we begin to unravel the mysteries of existence and embark on a transformative journey towards self-discovery. So, let us dive deeper into this realm of higher dimensions and unlock the treasures waiting for us there.

Connecting to Higher-Dimensional Beings

Right now, the Earth is undergoing energetic upgrades, which is called 'the ascension'. So many people are reporting contacts with higher-dimensional beings and, by connecting with them, you too can open yourself up to a whole new realm of possibilities. Whenever I connect to the Council they talk about peace, love and joy. Their message to us is always so clear: they want us to surrender lower consciousness thought forms and beliefs, and embrace forgiveness and unconditional love.

Through Incantation

One of the most common ways people attempt to connect with higher-dimensional beings is through incantation. When engaging in incantation, it's essential to approach it with sincerity, humility and an open heart. Begin by finding a quiet and serene environment where you can centre your thoughts and intentions. Create a sacred space where you feel comfortable and undisturbed, allowing yourself to enter into a state of reverence and contemplation.

As you begin your incantation, take a few moments to centre yourself through deep breathing or meditation. Clear your mind of distractions and focus your attention on the presence of the divine. You may choose to address your incantation to a specific deity, higher power or simply to the universe itself, depending on your spiritual beliefs and practices.

Express your thoughts, emotions and desires with authenticity and sincerity. Speak from the depths of your heart, articulating your intentions, hopes, fears and gratitude. An example of this is:

To the higher-dimensional beings around me, I call
upon your wisdom and guidance,
Illuminate my path with your divine light,
And lead me towards truth and insight.
With reverence and respect, I invoke thee,
To bless me with your presence and clarity.
May your cosmic energy flow through me,
As I navigate this journey of destiny.
So mote it be.

Trust that your words are being heard by the higher-dimensional beings, and that they are responding to your incantations with love, compassion and wisdom.

Be open to receiving guidance and insights during and after your incantation. Pay attention to any thoughts, feelings or intuitive nudges that arise within you. These may be subtle messages or signs from the spiritual realm, offering clarity, direction and comfort in response to your incantation.

Lastly, practise gratitude for the blessings and guidance you receive through incantation. Express appreciation for the presence and support of the higher-dimensional beings in your life, acknowledging their role in guiding you along your spiritual journey.

Through Mindfulness

You can also quieten your mind and open yourself up to receiving messages from these entities through deep concentration and mindfulness practices, such as journaling. By entering a state of heightened awareness, you can tap into the wisdom and knowledge that exists beyond our physical reality. It just requires practice and discipline.

Through Meditation

Whenever I have connected to a higher-dimensional being it has been through meditation. Meditation serves as a powerful tool for connecting with the universe and exploring the depths of our own consciousness – it is the key to moving through the dimensions. By quieting the mind and focusing inwardly, we create an environment conducive to receiving messages from beyond our earthly realm. Through this practice, you can have vivid visions and encounters with intergalactic beings who impart profound knowledge and guidance.

It is essential to approach such experiences with an open mind. The universe is vast and teeming with possibilities beyond our current understanding. Perhaps there are advanced civilizations out there willing to share their wisdom if we are receptive enough to receive it.

One form of meditation I do is something I call 'astral travel meditation'. This meditation technique involves deep relaxation and visualization, allowing the mind to separate from the physical body and explore other dimensions. Astral travel meditation is a powerful tool for spiritual growth and self-discovery. It will allow you to transcend your physical limitations and explore new dimensions of consciousness. Through regular practice, you can deepen your understanding of yourself and the universe around you. Through this practice, you can gain spiritual insights and connect with higher realms of consciousness.

To begin a meditation practice for connecting with other dimensions, find a quiet space where you will not be disturbed. I like to listen to a playlist that is instrumental, something I find relaxing – if this helps you to relax, you might like to do the same. Remember to have a pen and journal ready nearby.

Relaxation is key as any large emotions or
jolts can bring you out of the experience.

What I often find when I open my eyes is that I think I have been meditating for hours, when, really, it's only been 20 minutes.

Remember, successful astral projection adventures take time, patience and practice, so be sure to make it a regular habit if you want to leap to higher planes.

+ ⁺ ⁎ · ☾ · ⁎ ⁺ ⁺

ASTRAL TRAVEL MEDITATION TO HELP YOU CONNECT TO A HIGHER-DIMENSIONAL BEING

❯ Sit in a comfortable position and take a few deep breaths to centre yourself. Close your eyes and visualize a bright white light surrounding your body, creating a protective shield.

❯ Next, set your intention to connect with higher-dimensional beings who have your highest good in mind. This intention acts as a bridge between our world and the other dimensions we seek guidance from. It is crucial as it establishes the purpose of the connection – seeking wisdom and guidance for personal growth.

❭ Now, imagine yourself standing at the edge of a beautiful forest. Visualize the path leading into the woods as you take each step forward. As you walk deeper into the forest, feel the energy around you shifting, becoming lighter and more ethereal. During this experience, the astral body leaves the physical body and goes and explores other astral planes. The key here is to trust what you are sensing.

❭ As you continue walking along the path, pay attention to any signs or symbols that catch your eye. These signs may appear as glowing orbs or shimmering lights in various colours. Trust your intuition to guide you towards these symbols as they represent gateways to higher dimensions.

❭ When you reach one of these gateways or symbols, pause for a moment to observe its beauty and energy. Take note of any sensations or emotions that arise within you – these are indications that you are on the right track.

❭ Now comes the crucial part: opening yourself up to receive messages from higher-dimensional beings. Imagine yourself surrounded by an aura of pure love and light while affirming your openness to their presence. Ask questions silently or out loud if it feels more natural for you; inquire about specific areas in your life where you seek guidance. Be patient and receptive, allowing the answers to flow into your consciousness. These messages may come in the form of thoughts, images or feelings.

❭ Once you have received the guidance you sought, express gratitude to the higher-dimensional beings for their assistance. Visualize yourself walking back along the path through the forest, feeling a sense of peace and clarity.

❭ When you are ready, slowly open your eyes and return to your physical surroundings. Take a few moments to reflect on the experience and, in your journal, write down any insights or messages that came through during this exercise.

Connecting with higher-dimensional beings can be a transformative experience that expands our understanding of ourselves and the universe. By regularly practising this meditation, you can deepen your spiritual connection and gain valuable wisdom from these enlightened entities. Remember to approach this exercise with an open heart and mind – trust in the process and let it guide you towards greater enlightenment.

It is evident that this wisdom is not only accessible, but also freely available to all who seek it. It surrounds us, patiently waiting for us to tap into its power and manifest the life we have always dreamed of.

Through Dreams

You may also receive guidance from higher-dimensional beings through your dreams. Dreams are a gateway to the subconscious mind, where hidden truths and insights reside. It is believed that, during sleep, our minds are more receptive to external influences, allowing us to tap into higher realms of consciousness. In these altered states of awareness, contact with higher beings becomes possible.

Whether one believes in the existence of entities like extra-terrestrials or not, dreams and meditation offer unique opportunities for exploration and self-discovery. They provide avenues through which we can connect with higher realms of consciousness and potentially receive guidance from beings beyond our world. So, next time you find yourself dreaming or meditating, be open to the possibility that you might just be receiving messages from higher sources – messages that could unlock new dimensions of knowledge within yourself.

I know you've taken a lot on board up to this point, but I hope everything you have learned has opened your heart and inspired you. We all possess magic and wisdom within us that we can use every day.

As you journey through the dimensions, you're nearing the exciting initiation to fully embrace your inner witch in the next part!

PART V

Coming Home to Self

Welcome to the final part of your journey. You are about to dive into the different types of witches, how to create your own commitment to self as a witch and then the most exciting part, which is your initiation as a witch.

So, let's start your final coming home to self.

CHAPTER 15

Your Commitment as a Witch

As you embrace the path of witchcraft, questions may arise about whether you should adopt a specific 'title'. Terms like 'green witch' or 'cosmic witch' abound on social media, which can feel overwhelming. However, whether to claim a title or simply identify as a 'witch' is a personal choice. I'm here to guide you through the various types of witches, allowing you to choose which resonates with you, before you make a commitment to yourself as the witch you are becoming.

Types of Witches

There are so many different types of witches and modern witchcraft. As you read through this section, if you're drawn to a particular type of witch, trust your intuition and follow what feels right for you. It's perfectly okay if you feel pulled towards two or more types. Personally, I began as a Wiccan witch, but, as time went on, I identified more as an eclectic witch, blending traditional witchcraft with elements of green magic and divination. Remember, this journey is personal, and there's no right or wrong. Embrace what resonates with you.

Celtic Witch – many people still, today, honour the traditions of the Celtic witch through modern witchcraft practices that draw on ancient wisdom and symbolism. The Celtic witch is a figure steeped in mythology. She is a powerful symbol of feminine strength, wisdom and magic. The Celts believed that the natural world was alive with spirits and energies that could be harnessed for good or ill. This belief is rooted in pre-Christian religion and is popular with pagans. Celtic witches usually practise Celtic myths and rituals honouring their Celtic lineage. The Celtic witch works in group and individual rites, is able to communicate with the spirits of nature and uses her powers to heal and protect.

Ceremonial Witch – follows the traditions and rituals of ceremonial magic, working a ritual or ceremony into whatever they're casting or trying to accomplish. They sometimes call on higher beings and spiritual entities to assist them with whatever they're casting. Ceremonial witches believe in the power of symbols, ritual and invocation to connect with higher spiritual forces. They use tools such as wands, chalices and athames to channel energy and perform spells.

Cosmic Witch – often depicted as a wise woman who possesses knowledge of the stars, planets and other celestial bodies. They work with the stars and follow astrology, zodiac signs, horoscopes and celestial energy. They also work around the moon cycle. Cosmic witches use this deep knowledge to better understand themselves and others and to navigate life. In many ways, the cosmic witch embodies the idea of magic itself – an unseen force that can shape reality and transcend the limitations of our physical world.

This makes her a symbol of empowerment for those who seek to connect with something greater than themselves. The concept of the cosmic witch endures as a reminder of our connection to something greater than ourselves. She represents both the power and mystery of the universe, reminding us that there is always more to discover beyond what we can see or comprehend.

Coven Witch – a figure shrouded in mystery and superstition. As we explored in Chapter 1, throughout history, witches have been feared and persecuted for their supposed powers of magic and sorcery. The term 'coven' refers to a group of witches who gather to practise their craft. Coven witches are those who join together and engage in sacred ceremonies, rituals, healing, manifestations, spiritual work and witchcraft.

Crystal Witch – works with crystals, stones, rocks and gems. They use these in rituals and spell work to amplify energy and manifest their desires. They also work with energy vibrations and people's auras (*see pages 131-35*).

Divination Witch – they have been a part of human history for centuries. These witches are known for their ability to predict the future and provide insight into the unknown. They use various tools such as tarot cards, crystal balls, oracle cards, pendulums, scrying, palm reading, tea leaf reading and runes to gain information about the future.

Eclectic Witch – a practitioner of witchcraft who draws from various traditions and practices to create her own unique path. This approach allows for flexibility and personalization in one's spiritual journey, as the eclectic witch can choose what resonates with them and discard what does not. Many witches identify as eclectic, incorporating elements from Wicca, ceremonial magic, shamanism and other traditions into their craft. They may work with deities from different pantheons or create their own rituals based on personal beliefs.

Elemental Witch – the concept of an elemental witch has been present in folklore and mythology for centuries. These witches are believed to possess the ability to control the elements of nature, such as fire, water, earth and air. The elemental witch is often portrayed as a powerful figure who can harness the forces of nature to achieve their goals. Overall, an elemental witch continues to hold a powerful connection between humans and the natural world.

Faery Witch – a term used to describe a witch who practises magic in connection with the faery realm. This type of witchcraft involves working with the spirits of nature, including faeries, elves and other elemental beings. Faery witches believe that these spirits can help them connect with the natural world and bring about positive change in their lives. Faery witchcraft is often associated with Celtic mythology and folklore, as many of these stories feature faeries and other magical creatures. The practice involves rituals, spells and divination techniques that are designed to tap into the power of the faery realm.

Fertility Witch – represents our deep human connection to nature and our desire for abundance and prosperity. The concept of a fertility witch has been reclaimed by some modern practitioners of paganism and Wicca. Fertility witches are healers who work with natural energies to promote growth and vitality in all aspects of life. They work in traditional and holistic magic centred around the 'yoni' (the sacred feminine symbol representing the womb, vulva or female reproductive organs). They are knowledgeable about the ovulation cycle, maternal wellness, and baby- and childcare. Many of them are doulas or midwives or perform womb ceremonies.

Gardnerian Witch – worships the Goddess and Horned God, practising in a coven with an appointed High Priestess and High Priest. (The selection of a name for the Goddess is a deeply personal and spiritual decision, guided by individual intuition, connection and reverence for the divine feminine. Some common names used to address the Goddess include Aradia, Diana, Isis, Hecate, Brigid and Astarte. These names are often chosen based on the specific tradition or coven's preferences, beliefs or cultural influences.) Gardnerian witches follow the beliefs of the founder Gerald Gardner. In the 1950s, Gardner founded the earliest recorded Wicca (*see page 230*): the Gardnerian Wicca or Gardnerian witchcraft. Gardnerian Wicca is a modern pagan religion with its own belief system.

Green Witch – this type of witchcraft involves using plants, herbs and other natural materials to create spells and potions for healing, protection and divination. Green witches are often associated with the earth element and the goddess Gaia. They believe in living in harmony with nature and respecting all living beings. They also have a deep understanding of the cycles of nature, including the changing seasons and phases of the moon. Many green witches use their knowledge of herbs to create remedies for physical ailments or emotional imbalances. They may also use plants in their spell work to attract abundance or love into their lives. Green witches embody a deep connection to nature and a reverence for its power. Through their practice, they seek to harness this power for positive change in themselves and the world around them.

Hearth Witch – this is a term used to describe a type of witchcraft that focuses on the home and hearth. This practice involves using natural elements, such as herbs and crystals, to create a peaceful and harmonious environment within the home. The hearth witch also believes in the power of intention and visualization, using these tools to manifest positive energy within the household. The hearth witch is often associated with kitchen witchery, as cooking and baking are seen as sacred acts that can bring comfort and healing to those who partake in them. This type of witchcraft also emphasizes the importance of self-care, encouraging practitioners to take time for themselves and prioritize their own wellbeing.

Hedge Witch – also known as a solitary witch or a green witch, is a term used to describe a practitioner of folk magic who works alone and often lives on the outskirts of society. Hedge witches are typically associated with healing, divination and herbalism. The term 'hedge' refers to the boundary between the physical world and the spiritual realm. Hedge witches are believed to have the ability to cross this boundary and communicate with spirits and other entities. They use their knowledge of herbs, plants and natural remedies to heal both physical and emotional ailments. Hedge witchcraft has experienced a resurgence in popularity in recent years as people seek alternative forms of spirituality that connect them with nature. The practice emphasizes self-sufficiency, intuition and personal responsibility for one's own wellbeing.

Kitchen Witch – a practitioner of kitchen magic, which involves using food, herbs and spices to create spells and potions that promote health, happiness and prosperity. They believe that every ingredient has its own unique energy that can be harnessed for magical purposes. Their 'spells' are their recipes. In addition to their culinary skills, kitchen witches are also adept at divination and other forms of spiritual practice. They use their intuition to guide them in creating meals that are not only delicious, but also infused with positive energy. They are skilled in the art of cooking, herbalism and healing, and they use their knowledge to create a warm and nurturing environment for their families.

Lunar Witch – someone who uses the power of the moon and nature to manifest their desires and bring about positive change in their lives and those around them. They are practitioners of magic who draw power from the cycles of the moon. They place their tools, crystals or water outside to be energized by the moonlight. Lunar witches are attuned to the phases of the moon and use its energy to enhance their spells and rituals. The moon is believed to have a profound effect on human emotions, and lunar witches use this knowledge to influence their spells. Lunar witches are often associated with feminine energy, as the moon has long been linked to goddesses such as Artemis and Selene. They are also known for their connection to nature, using herbs, crystals and other natural elements in their practice.

Sea Witch – as the name suggests, a sea witch works with the ocean. However, they also work by harnessing the power of other bodies of water, such as lakes, rivers and streams. Sea witches will usually live close to water, as water will increase their power. They feel connected to ancient folklore involving sirens. They work by incorporating found materials like shells, sand, seawater, salt, seaweed and driftwood into their altars, rituals and spells. Some sea witches practise lunar and weather magic.

Shamanic Witch – a female shaman or medicine woman rooted in the ancient culture of paganism. Working with spells, rituals, initiations, counselling, herbalism and healing, a shamanic witch will often be seen working with drumming, dancing and plants to enter an altered state of consciousness.

Solar Witch – a powerful and mysterious figure in ancient mythology. She is said to possess the ability to harness the energy of the sun and use it to cast spells and perform magic. Solar witches time their rituals at sunrise or sunset when they believe the power of the sun to be most powerful. They work by harnessing the power of the sun and, just like a lunar witch (*see above*), they will charge their tools by sunlight instead of the moon.

Solitary Witch – a solitary witch who prefers to work alone rather than in a group. She is in complete control of her craft and makes her own rules.

Traditional Witch – practises the magic of their ancestors passed down to them through the matriarchal line and is dedicated to learning and practising the old ways of witchcraft. A traditional witch will work with magical practices and beliefs that were around long before religions such as Wicca existed. Traditional witches mainly hold ancient knowledge on spells, charms, talismans, rituals and herbal brews that date back centuries. They may combine this old wisdom with modern tools and ideas. A traditional witch can also be known as a folk or hereditary witch.

Wiccan Witch – Wicca is a modern religion based on nature and witchcraft traditions. Wiccans celebrate the Wheel of the Year (*see Chapter 4*) and focus more on ritual and less on religion. They worship both a goddess and god, representing the female and male aspects of our Earth. They have one 'rule', which is to not harm anyone with their magic.

Now that you've explored the diverse titles within witchcraft, I hope it's been inspiring and has helped you identify the path that resonates most with you. As a witch, consider what aspects of magic draw you in. Are you inclined towards herbalism, crystal work, divination or perhaps the magic of culinary arts? Take a moment to reflect on where your true interests and passions lie.

Embrace your journey with intention and commitment as you step into the magical realm. Trust in your intuition and allow your unique gifts to guide you along your path as a witch. With each step forward, may you deepen your connection to the craft and embrace the transformative power of magic in your life.

Your Commitment as a Witch

It's time to make your commitment to yourself as the witch you are becoming.

As you have discovered while you've worked through this book, to truly embrace the path of a witch is to embark on a deeply personal quest for authenticity, empowerment and connection with the natural world and all the dimensions within.

Cultivating a Strong Bond with the Natural World

As witches, we are not separate from nature; we are an integral part of it. By immersing yourself in nature's embrace, you can tap into the mysterious forces that govern the universe and channel your energy towards personal growth and transformation. The beauty of a forest or the crashing of waves can evoke an awe-inspiring sense of wonderment, stirring something deep within our souls. It is in these moments that we feel connected to something greater than ourselves – a force that transcends human comprehension.

Spending time outdoors, whether that is walking through woodlands or tending to a herb garden, allows you to witness first-hand the cyclical patterns of life and death that govern all living beings. It is within these present moments in nature that you can gain insight into your own existence and find solace in knowing that you are part of something much larger than your individual self.

By cultivating a strong bond with nature and aligning yourself with its rhythms, you can tap into its infinite wisdom and gain access to transformative energies that enhance your magical practice.

Honouring Yourself as a Witch

In our modern world, where distractions and external influences constantly pull us away from our true pure vibration, it is essential to find ways to return home to yourself. For those of us who identify as witches, this journey holds a profound significance as we seek to reconnect with our personal power and tap into the ancient wisdom that resides within us.

In a society that often encourages conformity and diminishes individuality, it becomes crucial for witches to engage in deep introspection. By reflecting on your thoughts, emotions and experiences, you can unveil your innate strengths, passions and desires. You will come face-to-face with past traumas and unresolved emotions that have held you captive for far too long, but take heart, through self-awareness you can reclaim your personal power and embrace an authentic existence that aligns with your core values.

> *Honour yourself and choose growth*
> *– that's living a magical life.*

Tapping in to Ancestral Wisdom

Being a witch is not merely about casting spells; it is a beautiful dance with history itself. To return home to yourself as a witch, you must go back in time and research your ancestors. It is here where knowledge of generations who have walked this path before you lies.

Unearthing this ancestral wisdom plays a crucial role in a witch's return home. By tracing back your lineage and connecting with ancestral spirits, you can gain access to ancient knowledge and spiritual guidance. The wisdom passed down from previous generations provides valuable insights into rituals, spells, herbal remedies, divination techniques and other magical practices. Through honouring these ancestral traditions, while adapting them to contemporary contexts, you can forge a meaningful connection with your roots while evolving your craft.

Through this communion with those who came before you – ancestral spirits reaching out from beyond to offer their guidance in this 3D world – you can honour their legacy while forging your own path; a path illuminated by ancestral wisdom and guided by spirits long gone, but never forgotten.

Working with Higher Dimensions

Working with dimensions is the ability to communicate with entities from alternate realities. These entities can take many forms, including spirits, deities and even beings from other planets or universes. By establishing connections with these entities, you can gain knowledge and wisdom beyond what is available in our physical realm.

As you learn to attune yourself to the flow of cosmic energy and align your intentions with the greater tapestry of existence, you will see your role as co-creators in this world. It is a journey that requires courage, vulnerability and an unwavering commitment to growth. Through introspection and contemplation, you will unlock the ancient wisdom that lies dormant within you, embracing your true essence as you return home to yourself.

As you reflect on all that you've learned and discovered, I encourage you to embrace your unique path and make a heartfelt commitment to your journey as a witch. Only by fully embracing this commitment can you move forward towards initiation in the final chapter, where you'll deepen your connection to the craft and embark on a transformative journey of self-discovery and spiritual growth.

CHAPTER 16

Your Initiation into Becoming a Witch

We have come to my favourite chapter, in which you will be initiated into becoming a witch. Initiation into witchcraft is a significant milestone in one's spiritual journey, marking the beginning of a lifelong commitment to understanding and harnessing the powers of the universe. I'm so glad you're here.

The initiation process varies across different witchcraft traditions, but it typically involves a series of rituals designed to test an individual's dedication, knowledge and ability to connect with the spiritual realm. These rituals are often shrouded in secrecy, passed down through generations within covens or small groups of practitioners. The initiation ceremony itself is a sacred event that symbolizes rebirth and transformation.

I want to guide you through how I initiated myself and, later in life, other witches, including my daughter. This initiation marks the beginning of a lifelong journey into self-discovery and spiritual growth. It involves undergoing a ritual to explore the mysteries of the universe while embracing your own innate power as a witch. The initiation into witchcraft is the taking of an oath or vow. This solemn promise signifies your commitment to follow the path of witchcraft faithfully and responsibly. It binds you to uphold certain ethical principles, such as doing no harm, respecting nature and using your powers for positive purposes only.

You can do this ceremony with witnesses or ask a witch to initiate you, or you can follow this guidance to initiate yourself. This process serves as both a purification ritual and an acknowledgement that embracing witchcraft requires leaving behind your old self.

Before I guide you to your initiation ceremony, I truly believe that, to step into a new energy and path, you must first clear away the old.

It is through the process of letting go that we create space for growth and transformation.

You have already gone some way with this process by examining your relationships and identifying whether there are any toxic connections that are draining your energy and hindering your progress. See Chapter 10 if you feel you need to do more work in this area. By acknowledging these unhealthy dynamics, you have made room for healthier connections that support your growth. Similarly, it is crucial that you have assessed your own thoughts and beliefs. Are there limiting beliefs holding you back from pursuing your dreams? By challenging these negative thought patterns and replacing them with empowering ones, you open yourself up to new possibilities. Look back at Chapter 9 for more guidance on this if necessary.

Clearing away the old also involves decluttering your physical environment. Our external surroundings often reflect our internal state. By organizing and tidying up your living spaces, you create an atmosphere conducive to clarity of mind and renewed inspiration.

Another way to clear away the old is to perform a break-free ritual:

BREAK-FREE RITUAL

Letting go can be challenging, as it requires us to release attachments to people, situations and beliefs that no longer serve us. However, it is essential if we want to move forward on our journey towards self-discovery and personal evolution. This break-free ritual will empower you to release these burdens, liberating your spirit and paving the way for new beginnings and transformative growth.

The perfect time for this ritual is: three days after a full moon.

TOOLS

For this ritual you will need the following items:

- tinfoil or greaseproof paper
- a small white spell candle
- coconut oil
- dried mint and lavender
- a small bowl of white salt: enough so that a candle can stand within the dish
- three dried bay leaves

> matches

> a cleansing tool such as incense or a smoke wand

> frankincense resin and a charcoal disc

> a cauldron or fireproof container

> a pen and a piece of A4 paper

> your journal

ℐNSTRUCTIONS

1. First you will need to prepare your breaking free candle. To do this, use the tinfoil or greaseproof paper as your surface. Using your finger, anoint your candle with the coconut oil. Then, sprinkle the mint and the lavender onto the tinfoil or greaseproof paper and roll the candle in it, towards you, so that the herbs stick to the candle.

2. Stand your candle up in the middle of the bowl of salt, then add the bay leaves to the salt.

3. Smoke-cleanse yourself, your tools and the space.

4. Light your charcoal disc and place it into your cauldron or fireproof container, adding the frankincense resin so you have a beautiful cleansing smoke. Frankincense produces a lot of smoke, so please open the windows.

5. On the piece of paper, write down what you want to release. Fold this paper away from yourself.

6. Light your candle and state the following:

I, [your name], release all beliefs and energy created
with or without my permission.
From this day in time I fully take my power back.
I call back my power.
I call back my power.

I call back my power.
As this candle burns without, it does so within, and so it is.

7. Place your hands around the flame and state:

    I fully let go of this, as this no longer serves me.

8. Now, offer your paper to the flames, placing it straight into your cauldron or fireproof container to burn.

9. Now, pick up the bay leaves and write a word on each, of your wishes that you are calling into your life about your new path as a witch.

10. One by one, offer these to the flame and drop them into the cauldron or fireproof container.

11. Once all burned, you can offer the cooled ashes to the earth outside.

12. Then sit back from the candle. Place your left hand on your heart and say, *So it is done, so mote it be.* Journal while the candle finishes burning.

$$+ \cdot_+ * \cdot_+ \cdot * \cdot_+ \cdot * \cdot_+ \cdot_+$$

Your Initiation Ceremony

Once you have performed the break-free ritual, you can start preparing for your own initiation ceremony.

Step 1: Pick a Date and Time

The first step is to pick a date and time of day that you would like to hold this ceremony for yourself. This could be a new moon, full moon or favourite season or Sabbath.

Step 2: Write a Commitment Letter to Yourself

Now, grab a pen and some paper and write a commitment letter to yourself to honour the path you are about to take as a witch. Once written, place this letter into an envelope and seal it. I have included an example below for you:

Dear Old Self,

I am writing this commitment letter to you as a declaration of my intention to become a witch. This decision has not been taken lightly, but, after much contemplation and soul-searching, I have come to realize that the path of witchcraft is calling me.

Becoming a witch is not just about casting spells or brewing potions; it is a spiritual journey that requires dedication, self-discovery and an unwavering commitment to the craft. It is about connecting with nature, harnessing its energy and using it for the greater good.

First and foremost, I commit myself to learning. I will immerse myself in books, ancient texts and teachings from experienced witches. I will study the history of witchcraft and its various traditions. By doing so, I hope to gain a deep understanding of the craft's origins and how it has evolved over time.

Furthermore, I pledge to honour nature in all its forms. As a witch, it is crucial for me to develop a strong connection with the natural world around me. I will spend time outdoors, observing the cycles of the moon and seasons. Through this observation, I aim to attune myself with nature's rhythms and learn how they can influence my practice.

In addition to studying and connecting with nature, I promise to cultivate my intuition. Intuition is an essential tool for any witch as it allows us to tap into our inner wisdom and make informed decisions. Through meditation practices and divination techniques, such as tarot reading or scrying, I will strive to strengthen my intuitive abilities. Through this meditation practice I will also strengthen my connection to all dimensions as we are all connected.

As part of my commitment, I vow never to misuse my powers or manipulate others through magic. Witchcraft should always be used responsibly and ethically. Any spell work or rituals performed by me will be done with pure intentions – whether that is to heal myself or others or manifest positive change in the world.

From this day, I commit myself to self-care and personal growth. Witchcraft is not just about external magic; it is also about inner transformation. I will prioritize my mental, emotional and physical wellbeing by practising self-love, mindfulness and engaging in activities that nourish my soul.

Lastly, I pledge to share my knowledge and experiences with others who are on a similar path. The witchcraft community thrives on collaboration and support. By offering guidance or participating in group rituals or gatherings, I hope to contribute positively to this vibrant community.

I understand that this path may not always be easy; there will be challenges along the way. However, with perseverance and unwavering commitment to my craft, I am confident that I can navigate through any obstacles that come my way.

So it is.

Love and gratitude,

My New Self

Step 3: Gather your tools

Now you are ready to gather your tools and begin your initiation.

If you wish to, put on your favourite outfit for the ceremony.

WITCH'S INITIATION CEREMONY

You can follow this guidance yourself or ask a witch to initiate you.

TOOLS

You will need the following:

- ❭ a broomstick or large tree branch
- ❭ matches
- ❭ herbal smoke wand or incense to cleanse yourself, the space and your tools
- ❭ your commitment letter
- ❭ Earth representation, such as a small bowl of earth or ash
- ❭ Water representation, which can be a glass of water
- ❭ Air representation, such as a feather to waft the smoke
- ❭ Fire representation, which is the power of a flame from a candle. Pick a new large white pillar candle
- ❭ a pen and small piece of paper
- ❭ a cauldron or fireproof container

Other optional tools include crystals, something that represents your ancestors, flowers and anything you feel called to add.

INSTRUCTIONS

When you are ready, cast your circle clockwise. This can be made by drawing with white chalk or a ring of salt or candles. Make the circle large enough to hold space for yourself and your tools.

1. Place the broomstick or tree branch outside of the circle.

2. Standing outside of the circle, do a grounding meditation to still your energy and return to your body.

3. Smoke-cleanse yourself, your tools and the space.

4. Place your tools (other than the broomstick/branch) and your commitment letter as an altar in the middle of your circle.

5. Standing outside of the circle once again, state out loud the following:

   A witch is a person in power. They are wise, they are a healer. They are aligned to the cycles of nature and to the phases of the moon. They understand the darkness and follow the light.

6. Place your left hand on your heart and state:

   I offer my body and soul to the spirits that be.

   Today, I welcome my old self into service of the triple Goddess and the Horned God as a witch. I call upon the Goddess and Horned God to witness this initiation.

   I, [your name], am about to dedicate myself as a witch. This is my commitment that should not be made lightly for this is for life and for my future lives to come.

7. Now, enter your circle.

8. Hold your commitment letter to your heart and state:

   As I speak these words of intent to the world and to the universe, I dedicate myself to the craft. In doing so, I open myself to the mysteries of magic and witchcraft.

9. Open your letter and read out loud your commitment. Then place this back on your altar.

10. Now you will anoint yourself to the spirits of the elements:

~ *Earth: with your finger, dab some earth/ash onto your third eye (between your eyes) and say, 'Power of earth, bless me with the gifts of strength.'*

~ *Water: drop some water on the top of your head and say, 'Power of water, bless me with the gifts of visions.'*

~ *Air: relight your smoke wand or incense and, using a feather, waft the smoke over yourself and say, 'Power of air, bless me with the gifts of honesty.'*

~ *Fire: light your candle and say, 'Power of fire, bless me with the gifts of love.'*

11. On the piece of paper, write the following: 'I let go of my fear of [a fear that you have carried with you that you wish to leave behind as you return home to yourself].' Now, offer this to the flame and place it in the cauldron or fireproof container to burn.

12. Say:

> *Blessed be my body, soul, mind and spirit. I return myself,*
> *[your name], home to the path of the witch.*
> *So it is done.*
> *So mote it be.*

13. Now leave the circle and jump/leap/step over the broomstick/branch.

After the ceremony, you can enjoy a favourite drink, dance or have a feast to celebrate. To close your circle, step inside and connect to your breath. Say out loud your gratitude for this space that has witnessed you and held you. Then clear it away. The candle can be blown out and relit every evening from that day forward, until it has gone.

Witch Re-Birthday

Once you have made this beautiful commitment to yourself, you can celebrate this witch re-birthday each year. For me, this date holds immense meaning and serves as a reminder to honour myself and embrace my magical journey.

On this special day, take a break from your usual routine and dedicate the entire day to self-love. It is a time for you to reflect on your first initiation into witchcraft, which marked the beginning of your path as a witch. Journal about areas where you feel you are perhaps slacking in your craft or aspects that you wish to explore further.

As you put pen to paper, write about how far you have come since your last witch re-birthday. Each year will bring new experiences, challenges and lessons that shape you as a witch. It is through these reflections that you can recognize the growth and progress made along this mystical journey.

Celebrate the knowledge you have gained throughout the year – spells cast successfully, herbs mastered, divination techniques honed – all contributing to your development as a witch. This celebration is not just about acknowledging achievements, but also recognizing areas where improvement is needed.

This annual ritual will allow you to reconnect with yourself on a deeper level and reaffirm your commitment to the craft. It serves as a reminder that being a witch is not just about casting spells or performing rituals; it is an ongoing process of self-discovery and continuous learning.

So, on our witch re-birthdays, let us embrace ourselves wholeheartedly, celebrating our unique paths as witches while acknowledging our growth and setting intentions for the future. May we always remember that self-love is an essential part of our magical practice – for only by loving ourselves can we truly harness our power as witches.

Conclusion

Returning home to oneself as a witch is not merely about acquiring knowledge or mastering spellcasting; it is an ongoing process of self-discovery and reclaiming one's authentic power. It requires dedication, patience and an open heart willing to explore both the depths within oneself and the vastness of ancestral wisdom. As witches embark on this journey of reconnection with themselves and their heritage, they become agents of change, not only in their own lives but also in society at large by embodying authenticity, resilience and compassion towards all beings – human or otherwise – fostering harmony between nature and spirit.

For me, witchcraft is simply a way of being, having a relationship with the world around me and seeing things in both a practical and spiritual way. Once I stood in my authentic self as a witch, I connected into my own power and became more confident. My words became chosen more carefully and consciously with less judgement. I began to seek others who shared my values. I learned how to manage my stress and I reconnected to nature. I found my magic by learning how to manipulate universal energy. I have learned how to use that universal energy by aligning my feelings with what I desire to happen.

*Being a witch is a part of you, not
something that you do.*

If you choose to believe anything, may it be in YOURSELF as you already have the magic! Your practice is personal to you and becomes your personality. You will begin to view the world differently.

You are not your past; you are not your fears; and you are not your darkness. Though life's challenges may seem insurmountable, light always pierces through the darkness. Embrace your desires and harness the power within yourself, for gratitude towards the shadows can lead to limitless achievements.

Trust your process. In those moments of doubt or fear, remember what is possible when you surrender it all – you find the magic that lies waiting for you, so that you become the alchemist of your life. Everything you need is already right there within you and around you, so allow it to guide you. Everything is working in constant harmony to return you back home to yourself, to your magic. Be the witch you have always been in lifetimes ago and into the future.

And so it is.

Acknowledgements

I would like to thank my husband Steve who has helped me throughout my journey and my two children Holly and Harry for their support and for being my inspiration.

I want to express immense gratitude to my Hay House team. A heartfelt shout-out to publicity director Jo Burgess, whose inspiration and gentle nudges have guided me profoundly throughout this journey. Special thanks to my editor, Kezia Bayard-White, for her unwavering support, enchanting touch and keen insight into my vision. And let's not forget the remarkable Julia Kellaway, editorial consultant, whose wisdom and integrity have been invaluable.

Gratitude to my coven of witches, my cherished sisterhood and my family for their unwavering support. A colossal thank you to every member of my social media community whose presence has contributed to making this dream a reality over the years! It's been an incredible blessing and privilege to share this journey with each and every one of you. Your presence is nothing short of magical.

About the Author

EMMA GRIFFIN is an eclectic, modern witch and intuitive channeler who was raised in a family of witches and mediums.

Globally recognized for her profound understanding of witchcraft, seasonal living, and her intuitive abilities, Emma empowers women to transcend doubts, fears, and self-sabotage; realign with their inner truth, power, authenticity, and purpose; and embrace a more enchanting life.

Central to Emma's mission is fostering a sense of sisterhood within communities. As a guiding light for women worldwide, her beautifully articulated guidance resonates with those navigating spiritual paths amidst the hustle and bustle of modern life. Emma's expertise in magical and spiritual development has garnered her acclaim, with appearances on esteemed platforms such as BBC, GB News, Talk TV and Heart FM, as well as the *Mirror*, *The Guardian* and UK festivals.

www.emmagriffinwitch.co.uk

@emmagriffinwitch

We hope you enjoyed this Hay House book. If you'd like to receive our online catalog featuring additional information on Hay House books and products, or if you'd like to find out more about the Hay Foundation, please contact:

Hay House LLC, P.O. Box 5100, Carlsbad, CA 92018-5100
(760) 431-7695 or (800) 654-5126
www.hayhouse.com® • www.hayfoundation.org

———

Published in Australia by:
Hay House Australia Publishing Pty Ltd
18/36 Ralph St., Alexandria NSW 2015
Phone: +61 (02) 9669 4299
www.hayhouse.com.au

Published in the United Kingdom by:
Hay House UK Ltd
The Sixth Floor, Watson House,
54 Baker Street, London W1U 7BU
Phone: +44 (0) 203 927 7290
www.hayhouse.co.uk

Published in India by:
Hay House Publishers (India) Pvt Ltd
Muskaan Complex, Plot No. 3,
B-2, Vasant Kunj, New Delhi 110 070
Phone: +91 11 41761620
www.hayhouse.co.in

———

Let Your Soul Grow

Experience life-changing transformation—one video at a time—with guidance from the world's leading experts.

www.healyourlifeplus.com

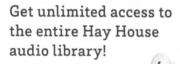

CONNECT WITH

HAY HOUSE
ONLINE

🌐 hayhouse.co.uk   **f** @hayhouse

📷 @hayhouseuk   𝕏 @hayhouseuk

▶ @hayhouseuk   ♪ @hayhouseuk

*Find out all about our latest books & card decks • Be the first
to know about exclusive discounts • Interact with our authors
in live broadcasts • Celebrate the cycle of the seasons with us
• Watch free videos from your favourite authors •
Connect with like-minded souls*

'*The gateways to wisdom and knowledge
are always open.*'

Louise Hay